GO

For almost a yea
deluged by reques
mailbags . . . vast flocks of carrier-pigeons (many of them so heavily loaded they have to come up in the elevator) . . . and at night the relentless pounding, pounding, pounding of jungle drums. Now, in answer to this avalanche of anxious requests, we are able to bring you good news!

DOCTOR LIVINGSTONE HAS BEEN FOUND!

He has been right here in the MAD offices all the time! Once that was settled, the editors wanted to celebrate with a new book. They have called it INSIDE MAD (in honor of the happy event) and it includes such amazing features as MICKEY RODENT! (a chilling tale of revenge), MOVIE ADS (fearless-type exposé), SMILIN' MELVIN!, THE KATCHANDHAMMER KIDS!, startling new facts about BAT BOY AND RUBIN!, fascinating PUZZLE PAGES, and much, much more!

Now the editors are relaxed again. They are contented (see picture below). They are happy and well fed. Only trouble is, once again Dr. Livingstone is missing.

THE **MAD** READER

MAD STRIKES BACK!

and now . . .

INSIDE MAD

written by

HARVEY KURTZMAN

drawn by

JACK DAVIS

BILL ELDER

WALLACE WOOD

with a special Backword by

STAN FREBERG

ibooks
new york
www.ibooksinc.com

DISTRIBUTED BY SIMON & SCHUSTER, INC

An ibooks, inc. Book

Distributed by Simon & Schuster, Inc.
1230 Avenue of the Americas, New York, NY 10020

ibooks, inc.
24 West 25th Street
New York, NY 10010

The ibooks World Wide Web Site Address is:
http://www.ibooksinc.com

Visit www.madmag.com

ISBN 0-7434-4480-9
First ibooks, inc. printing May 2002
10 9 8 7 6 5 4 3 2 1

Printed in the U.S.A.

CONTENTS

INTRODUCTION
by Grant Geissman

This book is a facsimile reprint of *Inside MAD*, the third in a new series of 50th-anniversary reprints–published by ibooks–of the early *MAD* paperbacks.

The original version of *Inside MAD* (released in December 1955 by Ballantine Books) followed *The MAD Reader* and *MAD Strikes Back!* (also available in facsimile editions from ibooks). Tracing the successful formula of its antecedents, it featured reformatted material that originally appeared in the twenty-three-issue run of the *MAD* comic book. As before, all of the material was written (and laid out for the artists) by *MAD* creator Harvey Kurtzman, and featured the core group of early *MAD* artists that included Wallace Wood, Jack Davis, and Bill Elder. Like *The MAD Reader* and *MAD Strikes Back!*, *Inside MAD* was a hit upon publication. Ballantine went back to press with the book in January 1956, and additional printings of it were ordered at approximately yearly intervals through 1964.

Continuing the practice of having well-known personalities contribute introductions to the *MAD* books (Roger Price wrote the foreword for *The MAD Reader* and Bob and Ray did the foreword for *MAD Strikes Back!*), Stan Freberg was enlisted to write the introduction for *Inside MAD*. Freberg was then enjoying great success with a series of comedy records (released on Capitol), including

"John and Marsha" (which consisted entirely of the words "John" and "Marsha" uttered at varying emotional levels) and "St. George and the Dragonet," a parody of the TV show *Dragnet*. Interestingly, Kurtzman had also taken on *Dragnet* as an object of satire (Kurtzman's parody, entitled "Dragged Net!," appears in the first volume in this series, *The MAD Reader*). This was hardly surprising; although the two satirists worked in different mediums, they were clearly on the same wavelength.

The opening slot in *Inside MAD* is occupied by "Mickey Rodent!," Kurtzman's look at Walt Disney's most enduring character, Mickey Mouse (*MAD* #19, January 1955, illustrated by Bill Elder). "Mickey Rodent" finds Kurtzman taking on the rivalry between Mickey Mouse and Donald Duck. Elder is at the peak of his game here; his aping of the Disney "house style" is deadly accurate. Elder's "signs in the background" technique is again in evidence, although in this case it's hard to tell where Kurtzman left off and Elder stepped in–signs that specifically advance the story are likely Kurtzman's. As Kurtzman develops his story, "Darnold" begins to smell a rat. Discussing "Mickey Rodent!," Kurtzman told comics historian John Benson that "in choosing my material, my starting point is within some popular subject where I detect a flaw or untruth. You recall when I did the thing on Walt Disney and Mickey Mouse–the three-fingered hand, the white gloves . . . it's a flaw in the sense that the public is accepting a three-fingered thing with white gloves. After all, let's not forget that Mickey Mouse is a huge, upright talking mouse, bigger than a giant rat." Note that at the very end of the piece, it takes but a single panel for Kurtzman to deconstruct Disney's entire anthropomorphic universe!

"Slow Motion!" originally appeared in a much longer form in *MAD* #21 (March 1955, illustrated by Jack Davis). Not only is the story truncated for its appearance here, but the opening panel has been reconfigured: in the original, a golfer is shown standing between the two cameramen, and the skier who appears in this version is not present (the ski image was taken from another panel in the story). "Slow Motion" is one of Kurtzman's "side by side" comparisons, this one showing the difference between what the naked eye sees and what the "slow motion" camera reveals.

Another of Kurtzman's "side by side" comparisons can be found in "Movie . . . Ads!" (*MAD* #14, August 1954, illustrated by Wallace Wood), which compares how scenes in movies are amplified to make them seem more exciting in the print advertising.

"Howdy Dooit!" (*MAD* #18, December 1954, illustrated by Bill Elder) takes on one of the best known and most beloved children's television shows of the 1950s, *Howdy Doody.* The show began on NBC on December 27, 1947, as *Puppet Playhouse with Howdy Doody*, and ran until 1960. The series spawned a merchandising bonanza, including such spin-off items as records, dolls, games, T-shirts, dishware, and even a popular comic book. Hosted by Buffalo Bob Smith (whose moniker came from his birthplace of Buffalo, New York) with his sidekick Clarabell the Clown and a cast of other recurring characters, the show also featured live commercials for the show's sponsors, Hostess Twinkies and Wonder Bread. Such direct advertising to impressionable children was later made illegal, and Kurtzman proves himself to be ahead of the curve here, inserting wry commentary on such practices throughout the story. Elder's art is nothing less than inspired, with his adorable-looking "Peanut Gallery" and endless background details. Note the "Less Work for Mother" tattoo on the arm of the "Peanut Gallery" handler in the second panel of page 45. Apart from the very first panel, in which the television set and the "Howdy Dooit!" lettering was in color (but not the image on the set), the story originally appeared in the *MAD* comic book in black and white to better simulate the black and white television that was then standard. Note that Kurtzman has also rounded off the edges of the panels to better simulate a television screen. As for the story's ending, it is classic Kurtzmania.

The "Canadian Specific," "Puntiac," and "Beer Belongs" ad parodies scattered throughout this book (*MAD* #22, April 1955) were originally part of a "Special Art Issue" that purported to showcase the life and work of *MAD*'s own Bill "Chicken Fat" Elder. In the issue, Kurtzman divided Elder's "life story" into sections: "The Child!," "The Boy!," "The Young Artist!," "The Commercial Artist!," and "The Old Pro'!" These ad parodies originally appeared in the "Commercial Artist!" section, and are notable in that they foreshadow the work both Kurtzman and Elder would do shortly thereafter in the magazine version of *MAD*.

Similarly, the one-page "Rubber Bubble Kids" (*MAD* #21, March 1955) is actually a small part of a much longer feature entitled "Comic Book Ads!," which spoofed the advertising typically found in the back sections of comic books, including such ads as "How to Hypnotize," "319 Stamps–All Different," and the "Red Ryder Cowboy Carbine." For these, Kurtzman had to look no further than the back pages of the comic books issued by *MAD*'s own publisher, EC Comics.

The charming and clever "Puzzle Page!" feature (*MAD* #19, January 1955, art by Bill Elder) that appears here and there throughout this book was originally part of one consecutive story (entitled "Puzzle Pages!," under the heading "Filler Dept."), and was reconfigured to suit the needs of the paperback format. "Puzzle Page!" sends up the many such one-page "fillers" that regularly appeared in vintage comic books. Not all of the original "Puzzle Pages!" story is present in this book, however; other parts of this piece appear in *MAD Strikes Back!*, the book that precedes this one in the series.

"Pop Art" version, late 1960s (Art credit unavailable)

"Smilin' Melvin!" (*MAD* #7, October-November 1953, illustrated by Wallace Wood) is Kurtzman's poke at the aviation/adventure strip *Smilin' Jack*. Created by Zack Mosely in 1933, it chronicled the adventures of Jack Martin, a suave, mustachioed commercial pilot whose routes took him on amazing adventures in faraway, exotic places. Among the cast of characters in the strip was Jack's sidekick Downwind Jaxon, a "chick magnet" whose face was so handsome he was never shown beyond a partial profile (parodied here as "Upwind Johnson"). After a long and successful run, *Smilin' Jack* finally had his last adventure on April 1, 1973.

Art by Robert Grossman (1975)

Another long-running (but now somewhat obscure) adventure strip, *Mark Trail*, gets the Kurtzman treatment in "Mark Trade!" (*MAD* #12, June 1954, illustrated by Jack Davis). Created in 1946 by Ed Dodd, the lead character was a somewhat unlikely one: Mark Trail was a woodsman and outdoor photographer who strove to preserve our forests and natural wildlife. Joined in his adventures by a lovable St. Bernard named Andy (spoofed here as "Sandy"), Trail's sensibilities actually predated the ecology movement by several decades. The specific sequence Kurtzman is lampooning here is one in which Trail was hired by *Woods and Wildlife* magazine to save some beavers in Sundance River County from poachers, and to photograph the process for publication in the magazine.

"Katchandhammer Kids!" (*MAD* #20, February 1955, illustrated by Bill Elder) is Kurtzman's treatment of *The Katzenjammer Kids*, widely regarded as the first true comic strip, and one of the longest-running features of any kind. The strip was created by Rudolph Dirks, and debuted on December 12, 1897. It centered on the antics of two incorrigible twins, Hans and Fritz, their long-suffering German-American Mama, and a cast of characters (Hans and Fritz's victims) that included the Captain—a kind of surrogate father to the boys—and "der Inspector," a truant officer. At the end of *MAD*'s send-up, Kurtzman takes the Kids' antics to their logical conclusion.

Art by Norman Mingo (1976)

"Bat Boy and Rubin!" (*MAD* #8, December 1953-January 1954, superbly rendered by Wallace Wood) is a classic and important early Kurtzman parody of Batman and Robin, and was Kurtzman's second look at characters from the DC Comics stable. *MAD* publisher Bill Gaines had already taken heat from DC's lawyers for Kurtzman's previous parody of a DC character, "Superduperman!" (see *The MAD Reader*), which prompted the "Notice! This story is a lampoon!" disclaimer in "Batboy and Rubin's" splash panel, lest DC again get the wrong idea.

"Shermlock Shomes!" (*MAD* #7, October-November 1953, illustrated by Bill Elder), sends up Sherlock Holmes, the classic and archetypal English detective created in 1887 by Sir Arthur Conan Doyle. Aided by his trusted friend Dr. Watson ("Whatsit"), Holmes's superior deductive abilities inevitably would allow him to outwit his arch enemy Moriarty ("Arty-Morty"). In coining the surname "Shomes" for this parody, Kurtzman was likely combining "Holmes" with "shamus," the Yiddish word for a detective or private eye. The Holmes character provided fertile enough material for Kurtzman to visit a second time in *MAD*; he tackled Doyle's *The Hound of the Baskervilles* (as "Shermlock Shomes in The Hound of the Basketballs") in a later issue of the *MAD* comic book.

It is gratifying (and even a little awe-inspiring) to note that the material that constitutes *Inside MAD*, originally published a scant three years after *MAD* made its debut in 1952 as a 10¢ comic book, is important enough to warrant this special 50th-anniversary edition.

Grant Geissman *is the author of* Collectibly MAD, *(Kitchen Sink Press, 1995), and co-author with Fred von Bernewitz of* Tales of Terror! The EC Companion *(Gemstone/Fantagraphics, 2000). He compiled and annotated the "best of" volumes* MAD About the Fifties *(Little, Brown, 1997),* MAD About the Sixties *(Little, Brown, 1995),* MAD About the Seventies *(Little, Brown, 1996), and* MAD About the Eighties *(Rutledge Hill Press, 1999). He compiled and wrote liner notes for* MAD Grooves *(Rhino, 1996), and also contributed the introduction to* Spy vs. Spy: The Complete Casebook *(Watson-Guptill, 2001). When not reading* MAD, *Geissman is a busy Hollywood studio guitarist, composer, and "contemporary jazz" recording artist with 11 highly regarded albums released under his own name.*

Foremost among the song parodists is a young Californian who has rocked the nation with such hits as "John and Marsha," "Try," and now "Rock and Roll Around Stephen Foster." You've seen his writing in Mad, Colliers *and other influential media. Now it gives us great pleasure to present this special Backword by Stan Freberg. Mr. Freberg . . .*

Well?

Where is he?

I don't see anybody.

Hold it. HOLD IT! You kids want to read Stan Freberg, don't you? Sure you do! Tell you what you do, then. Stan's Backword is around in the *back* of the book. Let's all turn to page 183 in our MAD books. Got that—page 183. Ready? Start turning!

INSIDE  MAD

Animation Dept.: Here is a thought! Who amongst you have seen the sight of man turned beast? A hapless few, we trust! . . . And yet . . . though we are repelled at the sight of man turned beast . . . we revel to see beast turned man! When you pass along this thought . . . remember you saw it in MAD! . . . And now, our story . . .

MICKEY RODENT!

...POOR HORACE HORSZNECK!
THEY'RE TAKING HIM AWAY FOR APPEARING WITHOUT HIS WHITE GLOVES!
... WELL YOU KNOW WALT DIZZY'S ORDERS ABOUT HOW WE'VE GOT TO WEAR WHITE GLOVES AT ALL TIMES...
... IN THIS HOT WEATHER TOO!
...AND IT'S SO HARD TO BUY THESE FURSHLUGGINER **THREE FINGERED** KINDS!
WELL...SO LONG, FOLKS! IF ANY OF YOU SEE **DARNOLD DUCK**, WOULD YOU TELL HIM I'M LOOKING FOR HIM?
O.K., MICKEY RODENT!
DOO IT!
WHY TV
PREVENT FOREST FIRES!
SMOKEY

WAAWA QUHI QUAY WIWIZZ QUOO QUO WAWA QUHIM...
HEY... DARNOLD DUCK!
CIRCUS 'FRITZ' THE BOY-FACED DOG!
QUHOO QUHWAWA QUHEE?*
HEY, DARNOLD DUCK!
* EDITOR'S NOTE: SINCE DARNOLD DUCK TALKS IN A QUACKING VOICE THAT YOU CAN HARDLY MAKE OUT, WE'LL MERELY PRINT THE TRANS-LATIONS FROM HERE ON IN!
BONG! ZZZIT
WALT DIZZY.
COPIED RIGHT! 1954 BY BILL ELDER.
1

GOONY! WHY DIDN'T YOU WARN ME ABOUT THAT BASEBALL!
I DID, DARNOLD! I KEPT YELLIN' FER YOU TO DUCK!
KING-SIZE PENCIL SET.
PET SHOP
NO PETTING ALOUD!
NO WONDER THEY CALL YOU GOONY! ...THE WAY YOU THINK... THE WAY YOU'RE DRESSED... YOU SURE ARE GOONY, BOY!
...THE WAY I THINK! ...THE WAY I DRESS! HAH!... YOU SHOULD TALK! YOU SHOULD TALK!... HAH!
SCHWEPPS ISH SCHWELL SCHODA

LOOK AT THE WAY YOU THINK! LOOK AT THE WAY YOU DRESS! HAH!... WOW! MOST EVERY DAY YOU WALK OUT DRESSED LIKE THAT! HOO BOY!
GULP!
CURB YOUR MORTAL!
...NEXT TIME YOU TALK ABOUT THE WAY I THINK!... THE WAY I DRESS... JUST MAKE SURE YOU HAVEN'T FORGOTTEN, AS YOU SEEM TO FORGET MOST EVERY TIME I SEE YOU...
...MAKE SURE YOU HAVEN'T FORGOTTEN TUH PUT ON YAWR PANTS!... (MOST SHAMEFUL THING I EVER SEEN!)
... BY THE WAY... MICKEY RODENT'S LOOKIN' FER YUH!

...MICKEY RODENT, EH? THAT OLD HAS-BEEN! FOLKS DON'T WANT TO SEE HIM ANY MORE!... I WISH HE'D QUIT HANGING AROUND!
HEY... DARNOLD DUCK!
"BEWARE OF HUMAN!"
BONG!
ZZZIT!
PEE KAN NEEZ
CHINEESE PAW LAUNDRY
WALT DIZZY
2

GOONY AGAIN! WHY DIDN'T YOU WARN ME!... WHY DIDN'T YOU TELL ME TO DUCK!
NOW HOLD ON, SON! I DID TOO TELL YOU TO DUCK!
...AND BESIDES.... I'M NOT GOONY! ...I'M PLUTED PUP!
WANTED DEAD OR ALIVE PUBLIC PEST NO. 1 MARK TRALE
...PLUTED PUP?! WELL HOW THE HECK AM I SUPPOSED TO HEAR A SIGN-BOARD THAT TELLS ME TO DUCK?

...CAN I HELP IT IF I CAN'T TALK? ...OH...BY THE WAY...MICKEY RODENT IS LOOKING FOR YOU!
NYAAH WHAT DOES THAT HAM WANT FROM ME?
... HE KNOWS DARNED WELL IT'S ME THAT PEOPLE WANT TO SEE... ME THAT KIDS TALK ABOUT! MICKEY RODENT'S ON THE WAY OUT!
ATTENTION BLOOD HOUNDS! BECOME A DONNER!
-IF YOU DON'T LIKE MY SIGN BOARDS, GO COMPLAIN TO WALT DIZZY.
...OH... THERE HE IS!
ATTENTION RABBITS! TAKE OUR CORRESPONDENC COURSE... LEARN TO SUBTRACT
...CAN I HELP IT IF OF ALL THE ANIMALS HERE... I HAVE BEEN CHOSEN TO RE-MAIN MUTE? WHY ME, I ASK YOU? AM I NOT AN ANIMAL LIKE THE REST OF YOU...

OH DARNOLD DUCK!
HABERDASHERY SHOP
SALE
COW SLIPS
HORSE COLLARS
TURTLE-NECK SWEATERS
ALLIGATOR SHOES
CATS PAJAMAS
MONKEY SUITS
DOGS PANTS
K-9
SPLAT!
... DARNOLD... IT IS I! **MINNY RODENT...** GIRL FRIEND OF MICKEY RODENT!
... WHY DID YOU THROW YOURSELF VIOLENTLY DOWN ON THE FLOOR WHEN I YELLED "DARNOLD DUCK"?
WALT DIZZY
3

...SOMEHOW... THE IDEA OF A MOUSE, WITH LIPSTICK AND EYELASHES AND A DRESS WITH HIGH-HEELED SHOES; A MOUSE, TEN TIMES BIGGER THAN THE BIGGEST **RAT**... THIS IDEA HAS ALWAYS MADE ME SICK!
UGH!
WHAT I WANTED TO TELL YOU, DARNOLD, IS ... MICKEY RODENT IS LOOKING FOR YOU!
"3 DUCKS IN THE FOUNTAIN."
HEY... DARNOLD DUCK...
WHY THERE HE IS NOW!
... HEY DARNOLD DUCK...
QUICK QUICK! YOU MEAN MY NAME, 'DUCK' OR YOU MEAN THE WORD, 'DUCK'?
YES BUT...
... THAT IS... YOU USE 'DUCK' CONNOTING **TITLE** RATHER THAN **ACTION?** ...QUICK!
YES BUT...

...THAT IS... 'DUCK' IS A VERB RATHER THAN A NOUN? TELL ME QUICK QUICK!
YES BUT...
...AHH!...THEN I CAN REMAIN STANDING!
REWARD
30,000,000 LUCKY BUCKS FOR THE CAPTURE OF 'BLACK BOOTY' THE HORSE THIEF. ..IS ARMED WITH A COLT!
DUCK PIN
BONG!
ZZIT!
YOU DIRTY ~~RAT~~ HUMAN! YOU SAID YOU CALLED ME... YOU CALLED ME BY MY FULL NAME!
...YES BUT YOU DIDN'T LET ME FINISH MY SEN-TENCE, WHICH, IF COMPLETED, WOULD HAVE BEEN... "HEY DARNOLD DUCK, DUCK!"
DUCK PIN

JUST LOOK AT THE **MOVIES** THEY MAKE... THE **BOOKS** THEY PRINT... DO YOU EVER SEE **HIM?** IT'S **ME** THE PUBLIC WANTS!... WHY DOESN'T HE SCRAMBOOCH TO THE OLD ACTOR'S HOME!
...NO HARD FEELINGS, DARNOLD!... SAY... IF YOU'RE GOING TO TOWN, LET ME GIVE YOU A LIFT IN MY CAR!
...WHEW!... IT SURE IS HOT TODAY!... SAY! LOOK OVER THERE, DARNOLD! LOOK AT THAT LITTLE SWIMMING HOLE HIDDEN AWAY OVER THERE... OVER THERE BY WALT DIZZY'S SIGNATURE?
...BY GEORGE... HE MUST DRAW PRETTY FAST!... I SEE HIS SIGNED CARTOONS **EVERYWHERE!**
...I SEE THE SWIMMING HOLE, AND YOU KNOW ME!... I TAKE TO WATER LIKE A DUCK TAKES TO WATER!
WALT DIZZY
WD1
4

HAW!... LIKE A DUCK TAKES TO WATER?...OH YOU FOOL... HOW CAN YOU EVER HOPE TO COMPETE WITH SUCH AS I!
WE'LL TAKE OFF OUR CLOTHES AND LEAVE THEM BEHIND THESE BUSHES WHILE WE GO SWIMMING!
COME NOW, MICKEY RODENT... AREN'T YOU GOING TO TAKE OFF YOUR GLOVES?
...I CAN'T!...YOU SEE...I HAD THEM TATOOED ON A LONG TIME AGO!
...WHEE! AIN'T THIS FUN!
LOOK... NO HANDS! ...THAT IS... NO WINGS!...I MEAN, NO HAND-WINGS!... I MEAN...
WANTED- LIFE SAVERS. ALL KINDS FLAVORS!

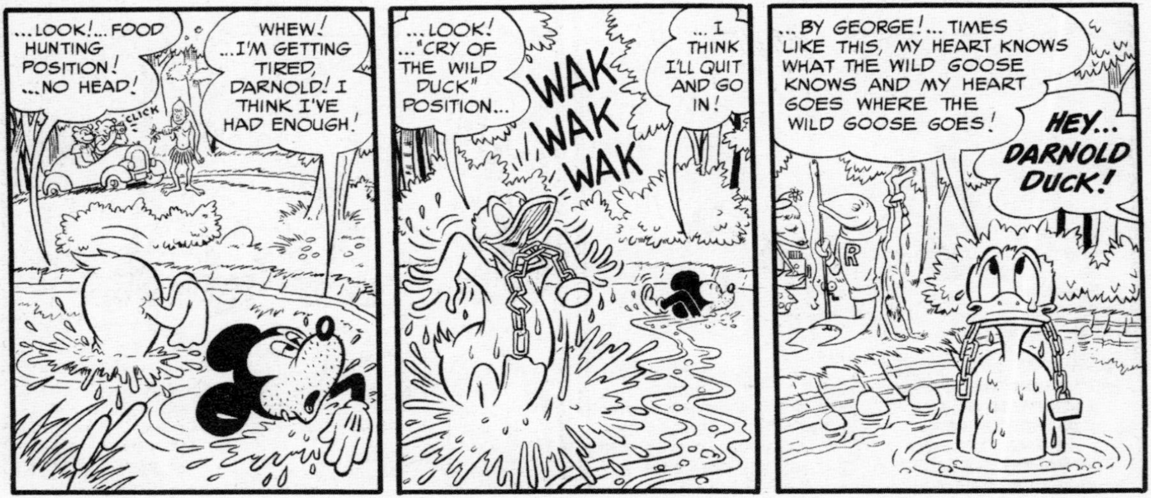
...LOOK!...FOOD HUNTING POSITION! ...NO HEAD!
CLICK
WHEW! ...I'M GETTING TIRED, DARNOLD! I THINK I'VE HAD ENOUGH!
...LOOK! ..."CRY OF THE WILD DUCK" POSITION...
WAK WAK WAK
... I THINK I'LL QUIT AND GO IN!
...BY GEORGE!... TIMES LIKE THIS, MY HEART KNOWS WHAT THE WILD GOOSE KNOWS AND MY HEART GOES WHERE THE WILD GOOSE GOES!
HEY... DARNOLD DUCK!

GOOSH

KID...ANYTIME I'M ON THE GOOD OLD AQUA-PURA... YOU CAN YELL FOR ME TO DUCK!... ANYTIME I'M ON THE GOOD OLD WATEROLA, KID...
LISTEN, DARNOLD... OUR CLOTHES! ...THEY'RE GONE! ...WHILE WE WENT SWIMMING, SOMEBODY STOLE OUR CLOTHES!
BOY AM I LUCKY I DIDN'T TAKE OFF MY TATOOED GLOVES!
WALT DIZZY
5

WHAT?... ONE OF THE FEW TIMES I MANAGED TO WEAR MY PANTS AND SOMEBODY STOLE THEM?... I DON'T LIKE THE LOOKS OF THIS!
LOOK!... FOOTPRINTS OF A PEG-LEG!... IT MUST BE MY OLD ARCH ENEMY... PEG-LEG POOP WHO STOLE OUR CLOTHES! ... LET'S FOLLOW THE TRACKS!
Eat at JOE'S BAR-B-Q 1000 FT. AHEAD
DO NOT PICK!
LOOK!... THEY GO STRAIGHT AHEAD THROUGH THE TREES! ... COME ON!
I DON'T LIKE THE LOOKS OF THIS!... IT'S GETTING DARK AND I DON'T LIKE THE STYLE THIS SCENERY IS GETTING!... HAH!... LOOK AT THAT SIGNATURE! IT'S NOT WALT DIZZY'S STYLE. ...I KNEW THE STYLE OF THIS DRAWING WAS DIFFERENT!
JOE'S BAR-B-Q 50 FT. AHEAD
BILL ELDER.

SEE... THE STYLE OF DRAWING IS ALL WITH SHADING... NO SIMPLE OUTLINES LIKE WE USUALLY HAVE... AND... AND LOOK! ... THIS PROVES IT! SOMETHING'S SCREWY! ... WE'VE NOW GOT **FIVE** FINGERS ON EACH HAND!
...THE FOOTSTEPS GO THROUGH THIS GATE! ...GO AHEAD, DARNOLD!
JOE'S BARB.

CLANG!
PLEASE CLOSE DOOR: AVOID DRAFTS!

NOW I'VE GOT YOU WHERE I WANT YOU, DARNOLD DUCK! PEG-LEG POOP DIDN'T TAKE YOUR CLOTHES! I DID! IT WAS ALL PART OF MY PLAN TO GET YOU HERE!... FOR YEARS I'VE BEEN PLANNING THIS!
...FOR YEARS I'VE WATCHED YOU PUSHING YOUR WAY INTO MY ACT!... FOR YEARS I'VE WATCHED HOW YOU'VE COME! ...YOU AND YOUR BLASTED RELATIVES... THEM THREE LITTLE NOODNIK DUCKS!... I'VE SEEN YOU SLOWLY HUSTLING ME OUT OF THE PICTURE!... WELL I'M PUSHING YOU OUT, HERE AND NOW!
YOU THINK YOU CAN SHUT ME OUT WITH A GATE... WITHOUT MY CLOTHES? ...I'LL GET BACK, BOY! I'LL GET BACK, SHVIENHUNT... I MEAN SHVEINMOUSE!
WE'LL SEE IF YOU GET BACK!... WE'LL SEE...

CHIEF CURATOR
PROFESSOR! PROFESSOR! COME WITH ME QUICKLY!
WHAT IS IT, MAN?
IN MY TEN YEARS HERE, I'VE NEVER SEEN ANYTHING LIKE THIS, SIR!
...I CAN'T IMAGINE WHAT IN THE WORLD YOU ARE TALKING ABOUT!

WELL, I HAD JUST FINISHED PREPARING THE CORN-MASH AND WAS MAKING MY ROUNDS...
UM HUM!
THERE IT WAS, STANDING WITH THE REST OF THEM...
OH HO?
...CAN'T UNDERSTAND WHY I'D NEVER NOTICED IT BEFORE WHILE MAKING THE ROUNDS...
AH HAH!

...AND...OH! HERE WE ARE!... SEE IT?... THE ONE SORT OF COWERING AGAINST THE BACK WALL?
HMPF! OBVIOUSLY SOME SORT OF MUTATION FREAK! THE ZOOLOGICAL SOCIETY WILL GET A MILD LAUGH OUT OF THAT SPECIMEN!
...IT WAS SQUAWKING ALL OVER THE DUCK'S CAGE BEFORE AND FUNNY THING!... IT ALMOST SOUNDED LIKE IT WAS TALKING... LIKE IT WAS SAYING "GET ME BACK MY CLOTHES," OR SOMETHING!
WELL... IF IT GETS TOO UN-MANAGEABLE...WE CAN ALWAYS PRESERVE BY STUFFING IT!
...AFTER ALL... IT IS ONLY A DUCK!
7

For a world of service, travel Canadian Specific. Canadian Specific's 4-engined pressurized airliners fly from Canada to Hawaii, Fiji, New Zealand, Australia, Belgian Congo, Tibet, the North Pole, the Kremlin, the Moon and Kukamonga. By George! We take you anywhere! Canadian Specific's engined pressurized airliners have the straightest lines trailing out in back of the airplane drawings in their ads then any other airline.

Canadian Specific

SPANS THE WORLD

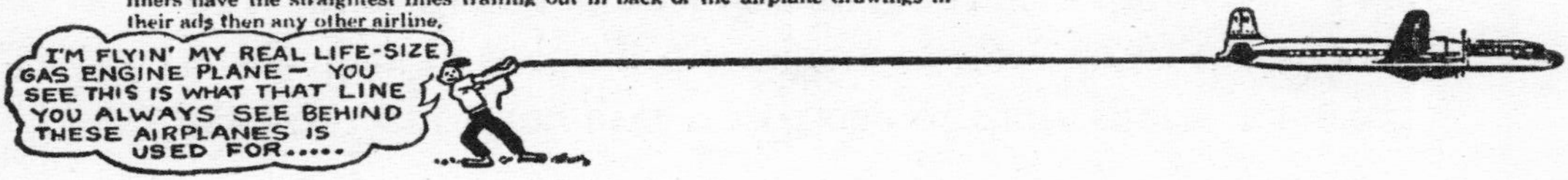
I'M FLYIN' MY REAL LIFE-SIZE GAS ENGINE PLANE — YOU SEE THIS IS WHAT THAT LINE YOU ALWAYS SEE BEHIND THESE AIRPLANES IS USED FOR.....

Science Dept.: You ever watch one of those sports newsreels where they've sped up the camera to slow down the action? By George, there's more going on than meets the eye! . . . Like forinstance, let us show you what happens to a ski jumper coming off the end of the jump . . . as seen by our camera in . . .

SLOW MOTION!

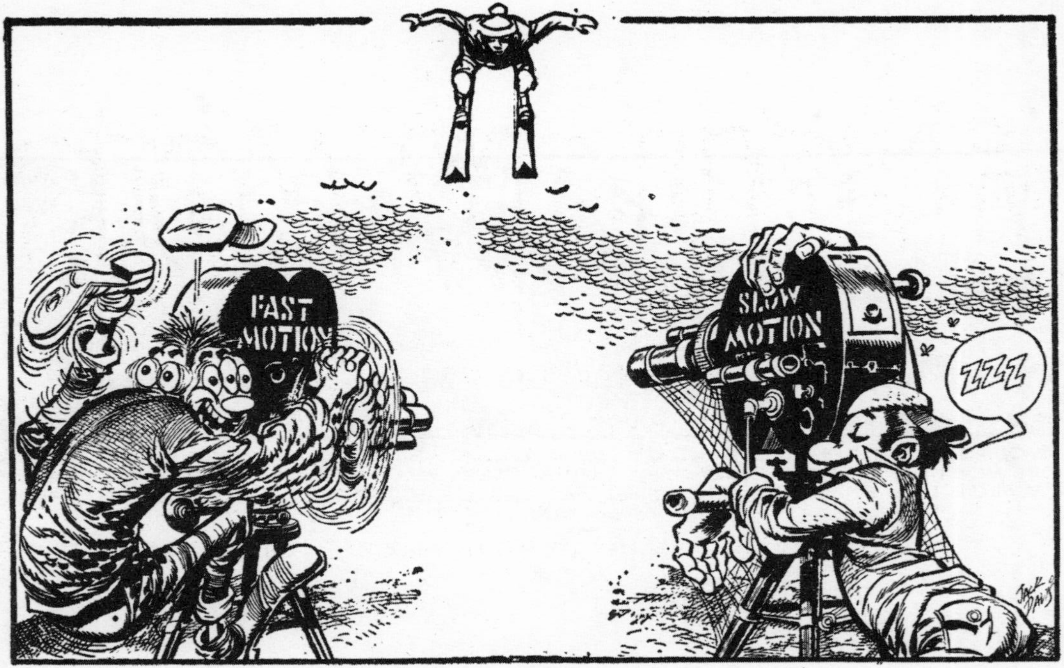
FAST MOTION
SLOW MOTION
ZZZ
JACK DAVIS

SKIERS ARE PROBABLY CRAZY, BUT WE'VE GOT SO USED TO WATCHING THEM THAT WE THINK NOTHING OF SEEING THE SKIER FLY THROUGH THE AIR AND FALL HUNDREDS OF FEET!
...WE THINK NOTHING OF SEEING HIM LAND IN A BIG FLURRY OF SNOW!... LITTLE DO YOU KNOW WHAT THINGS GO ON IN THAT BIG FLURRY OF SNOW!

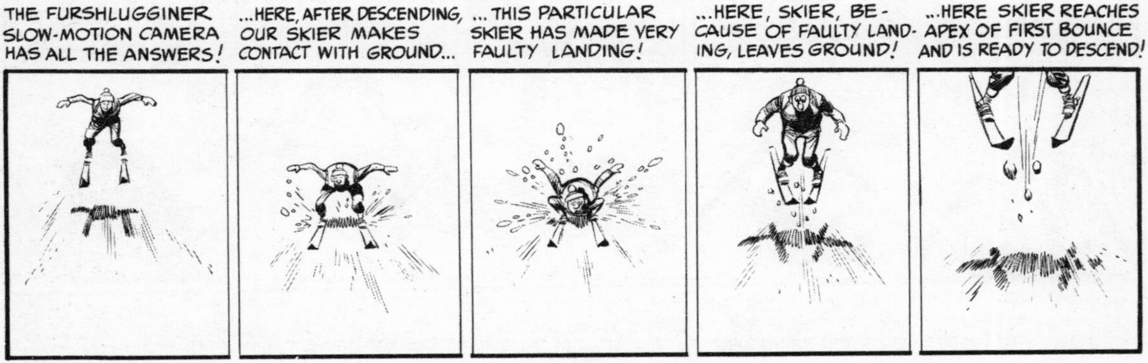
THE FURSHLUGGINER SLOW-MOTION CAMERA HAS ALL THE ANSWERS!
...HERE, AFTER DESCENDING, OUR SKIER MAKES CONTACT WITH GROUND...
... THIS PARTICULAR SKIER HAS MADE VERY FAULTY LANDING!
...HERE, SKIER, BE-CAUSE OF FAULTY LAND-ING, LEAVES GROUND!
...HERE SKIER REACHES APEX OF FIRST BOUNCE AND IS READY TO DESCEND!

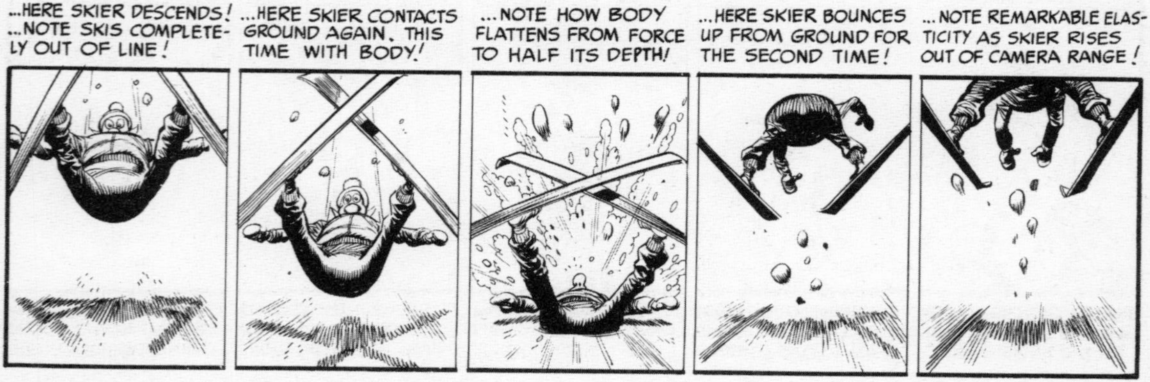
...HERE SKIER DESCENDS! ...NOTE SKIS COMPLETELY OUT OF LINE!
...HERE SKIER CONTACTS GROUND AGAIN. THIS TIME WITH BODY!
...NOTE HOW BODY FLATTENS FROM FORCE TO HALF ITS DEPTH!
...HERE SKIER BOUNCES UP FROM GROUND FOR THE SECOND TIME!
...NOTE REMARKABLE ELASTICITY AS SKIER RISES OUT OF CAMERA RANGE!

...NOTE FOR MOMENT WHILE SKIER IS OUT OF PICTURE, DEEP GOUGES IN SNOW!
...NOTE SKIER DESCENDS INTO PICTURE AGAIN, THIS TIME HEAD FIRST!
...NOTE HEAD ABOUT TO CONTACT GROUND WITH GREAT FORCE!
...NOTE FORCE WITH WHICH SNOW AND ROCKS ARE FLUNG FROM IMPACT!
...NOW NOTE SEPARATE PARTS OF SKIER AS THEY BOUNCE UP FOR LAST TIME!
5

TV Dept.: Our constant readers have no doubt noticed our sudden shift to television! We are giving special attention to TV because we believe it has become an integral part of living . . . a powerful influence in shaping the future . . . but mainly we are giving attention because we just got a new TV set! So here's our story . . .

HOWDY DOOIT!

NO! LET ME GO! THAT'S MY SUNRAY FROM MY MOVIES BEHIND HIS HEAD AND I WANNIT BACK!
BILL Elder
BREAK THE BANK
KIDDIE PROGRAMS
LIBERACE
DIAL "M" FOR MURROW
THE BUTTONS SHOW

HEY KIDS...
POW
SOK
...WHAT TIME IS IT?
HEY SHLOIMY!
THE PHANTOM SPITTER WAS HERE!

I DON'T KNOW WHAT TIME IS IT?
YOU KNOW WHAT TIME IS IT?
ANYBODY KNOW WHAT TIME IS IT?
...DINNER TIME IS IT?
...IS NAP TIME?
I DON'T HAVE A WATCH, MISTER!
I NO NO WHAT TIME IS IT!
...BATH TIME?
...TIME MAGAZINE?
HEY SHLOIM- WHAT TIME IT IS?
TSST! ...IT'S HOWDY DOOIT TIME!
TSST! ANSWER IT'S HOWDY DOOIT TIME!
TSST!

THAT'S RIGHT, KIDS!... IT'S HOWDY DOOIT TIME!
...AND THIS IS...
BIGELOW 2-3467

...THE PEEWEE GALLERY!!!
C'MON! YOK IT UP, KIDS!
YAY
THAT'S IT, KIDS! REALLY YOK IT UP!
MORE!
MORE!
THAT'S IT!
YAY
...THAT'S IT, KIDS!
...O.K.! THAT'S ALL!
RAY

THAT'S ALL, KIDS!
...THERE WE GO, KIDS!
...KIDS!
FINISHED, KIDS!
...THE END!
ALL THROUGH, KIDS!
CUT IT OUT, KIDS!
STOP!
SHUDDUP!
...KIDS...
GAAAAAAAH!
DUE TO TECHNICAL DIFFICULTIES YOUR PICTURE WILL BE TEMPORARILY DELAYED! PLEASE STAND BY...
Thank you—
2

HI, KIDS! NOW ***HOWDY DOOIT*** WANTS TO TAKE TIME OUT FOR A LITTLE COMMERCIAL!... KIDS! I HAVE A MESSAGE FOR YOUR MOTHERS... SO WOULD YOU PLEASE GO INTO THE KITCHEN AND CALL MOM TO THE TELEVISION SET?
DIDN'T YOU HEAR ME... YOU STILL SITTING THERE!? ...GET OUT AND CALL YOUR MOTHERS!
GET GOING BEFORE I GET MAD!
HISSS!

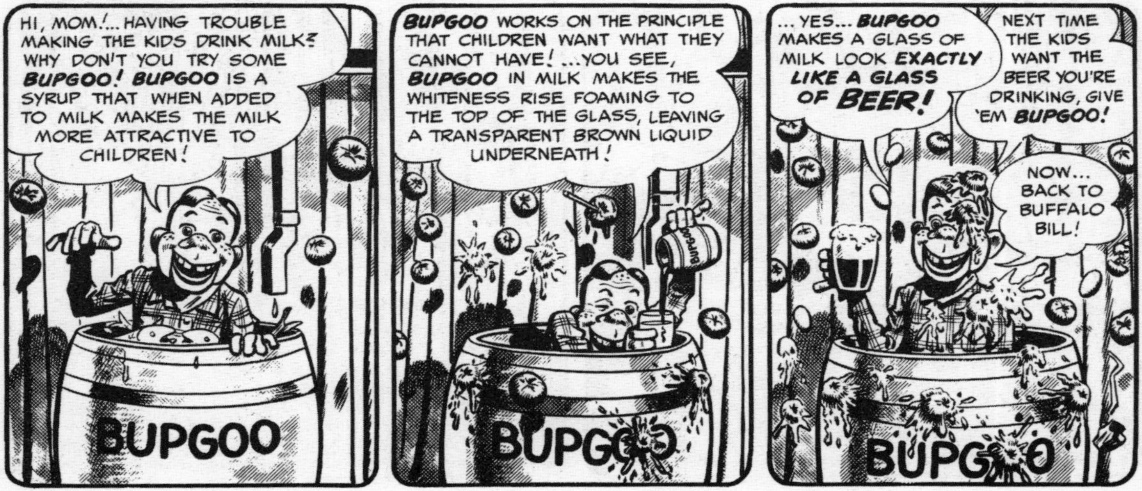
HI, MOM!... HAVING TROUBLE MAKING THE KIDS DRINK MILK? WHY DON'T YOU TRY SOME BUPGOO! BUPGOO IS A SYRUP THAT WHEN ADDED TO MILK MAKES THE MILK MORE ATTRACTIVE TO CHILDREN!
BUPGOO
BUPGOO WORKS ON THE PRINCIPLE THAT CHILDREN WANT WHAT THEY CANNOT HAVE! ...YOU SEE, BUPGOO IN MILK MAKES THE WHITENESS RISE FOAMING TO THE TOP OF THE GLASS, LEAVING A TRANSPARENT BROWN LIQUID UNDERNEATH!
BUPGOO
BUPGOO
...YES... BUPGOO MAKES A GLASS OF MILK LOOK EXACTLY LIKE A GLASS OF BEER!
NEXT TIME THE KIDS WANT THE BEER YOU'RE DRINKING, GIVE 'EM BUPGOO!
NOW... BACK TO BUFFALO BILL!
BUPGOO

HOW, BIG CHIEF THUNDAMELVIN!...STILL HIDING YOUR MUSTACHE UNDER THAT WARPAINT, YOU RASCAL YOU?
...KOWABUNGA, BUFFALO BILL...ME LOOKIN' FOR CLARABELLA! THERE SOMETHING BOTHERING ME FOR LONG TIME! ...ME WANT TO ASK CLARABELLA!
WHY... HERE COMES CLARABELLA NOW!
GOSHAROOTIE... I MEAN **KOWABUNGA**, CLARABELLA! IS SOMETHING ME GOTTUM ASKUM YOU! ME KNOW FACE OF CLOWN OFTEN COVER GREAT WISDOM! WISDOM MANY TIME LAY UNDER SENSE OF HUMOR! ME WANT ASK YOU ONE QUESTION EVER SINCE ME MEET YOU! EVER SINCE ME HEAR YOUR NAME, **CLARABELLA** ME WANT TO ASK...
I LIKE IKE
MACY'S PARADE
3

...IS YOU A WOMAN?
I LIKE IKE

KOWABUNGA! HIM GOT WOMAN'S **NAME!** IF HIM **MAN,** WHY HIM GOT WOMAN'S **NAME?** ALL I WANT IS THE FACK'S... WHICH REMIND ME... HOW'S YOUR MOM, ED?
LET'S GET OUT OF HERE! YOU KNOW WHAT CLARABELLA'S GOT IN THAT BOX HE CARRIES! ...YOU KNOW WHAT CLARABELLA'S ABOUT TO DO!
CLARABELLA
I LIKE IKE

IT'S NO USE! HE'S ALREADY WHIPPING THOSE THINGS OUT OF THAT BOX!... HERE COMES THE SELTZER BOTTLE!... WE MIGHT AS WELL STAND AND MEET OUR FATE!
CLARABELL

...GOSH... WHAT'S GOING TO HAPPEN NEXT? WELL, KIDS! IT'S ME, **HOWDY DOOIT** AGAIN AND THIS TIME I'M ADVERTISING **SKWUSHY'S** SLICED WHITE-BREAD! NOW LISTEN, KIDS... THE NEXT TIME YOUR MOTHER GOES TO THE STORE, I WANT YOU TO ASK HER TO BUY A LOAF OF **SKWUSHY'S!**
HALF-BAKED WHILE YOU SLEEP!
SKWUSHY'S *
* A WONDER PRODUCT: "IF IT'S GOOD BREAD-IT'S A WONDER!"

NOW IN CASE YOUR MOTHER REFUSES TO BUY YOU A LOAF OF SKWUSHY'S, HERE'S WHAT TO DO! NOW MAKE BELIEVE I'M YOU AND MAKE BELIEVE THAT'S YOUR MOTHER SHOPPING IN THE SUPER-MARKET AND SHE DOESN'T WANT TO BUY BREAD TODAY!
... YOU JUST WAIT TILL HER BACK IS TURNED AND SLIP A LOAF OF SWUSHY'S INTO THE SHOPPING BASKET!...HIDE IT WAY UNDER WHERE SHE CAN'T NOTICE IT!... THEN AGAIN... IF MOM HAPPENS TO BUY ANOTHER BRAND OF BREAD...
STERNO
ZIP!
... WAIT TILL SHE GETS STUCK ON THE LINE AT THE CASHIER'S COUNTER AND QUICK SUBSTITUTE A LOAF OF SKWUSHY'S! SHE'LL HAVE TO BUY IT!... BESIDES SKWUSHY'S WHITE BREAD, TRY SKWUSHY'S GREEN AND PURPLE BREAD!
ZIP!
4

...NOW BACK TO OUR STORY!
IT'S NO USE! HE'S ALREADY WHIPPING THOSE THINGS OUT OF THAT BOX!... HERE COMES THE SELTZER BOTTLE!... WE MIGHT AS WELL STAND AND MEET OUR FATE!
CLARABELLA

NOW YOU KNOW IT AIN'T RIGHT TO SQUIRT SELTZER, CLARABELLA!
...ESPECIALLY TO SQUIRT SELTZER ON TELEVISION!
ESPECIALLY TO SQUIRT SELTZER ON THIS TYPE PROGRAM!
... AND ***MAINLY*** ESPECIALLY TO SQUIRT SELTZER ON SCOTCH!
BEEP BEEP
CLA

EXCUSE ME AGAIN, KIDS, BUT I WANT TO TELL YOU ABOUT **PHUD** CEREAL FLAKES! **PHUD** CEREAL FLAKES DON'T SNAP, CRACKLE OR POP! **PHUD** JUST LAYS THERE IN THE BOWL IN ONE SOGGY MESS!... NOW KIDS, LET ME SUGGEST HOW YOU CAN GET YOUR MOM TO BUY **PHUD**!
PHUD
" THE BREAKFAST OF CHIMPANZEES."
~ALSO A MILD DETERGENT
PHUD
...IF MOM WON'T BUY YOU **PHUD**, YOU JUST STAND IN THE NEXT ROOM AND YELL LIKE THIS...
I WAN' IT! I WAN' IT! I WAN' IT! I WAN' IT! I WAN' IT!

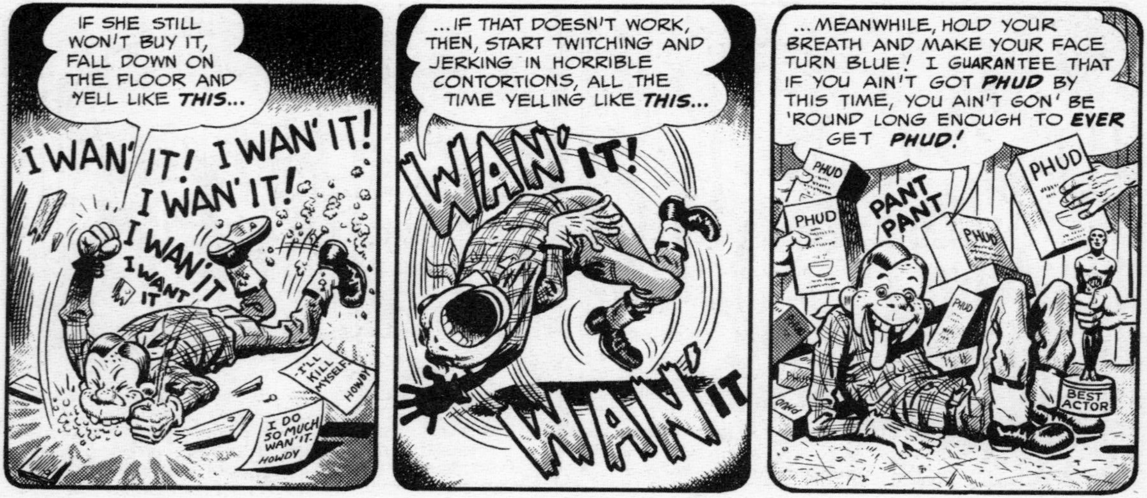
IF SHE STILL WON'T BUY IT, FALL DOWN ON THE FLOOR AND YELL LIKE **THIS**...
I WAN' IT! I WAN' IT!
I WAN' IT!
I WAN' IT
I WANT IT
I'LL KILL MYSELF. HOWDY
I DO SO MUCH WAN' IT. HOWDY
...IF THAT DOESN'T WORK, THEN, START TWITCHING AND JERKING IN HORRIBLE CONTORTIONS, ALL THE TIME YELLING LIKE **THIS**...
WAN' IT!
WAN' IT
...MEANWHILE, HOLD YOUR BREATH AND MAKE YOUR FACE TURN BLUE! I GUARANTEE THAT IF YOU AIN'T GOT **PHUD** BY THIS TIME, YOU AIN'T GON' BE 'ROUND LONG ENOUGH TO **EVER** GET **PHUD**!
PANT PANT
PHUD
BEST ACTOR

O.K., KIDS! NOW COMES THE PART WHERE WE INTERVIEW THE CHILDREN IN THE PEEWEE GALLERY!... DID YOU EVER SEE SUCH A NICE BUNCH OF WELL-BEHAVED KIDS?

YESSIR...A SWELL BUNCH OF NICE, WELL-BEHAVED KIDS... **OOP...**
TSST!... MOVE THE CAMERA BACK!... TSST! GET THE GUARD OFF CAMERA!... TSST...
LESS WORK FOR MOTHER

THE QUESTION FOR TODAY IS: WHAT WOULD YOU LIKE TO BE WHEN YOU GROW UP?
AH THERE! HERE'S A BRIGHT YOUNG LADY!... WHAT WOULD YOU LIKE TO BE WHEN YOU GROW UP, HONEY?
...UH, WHAT I'D LIKE TO BE WHEN I GROW UP IS...WHAT I'D LIKE TO BE IS...
BETTER BUY BOIDS EYE!
...IS SIX FEET! ...MAYBE SIX FEET TWO! MAYBE SIX FEET ONENA-HALF!...
MAYBE SIX FEET ONE! ...MAYBE JUS' SIX FEET! SIX FEET ONENA-HALF'S O.K.! SIX FEET TWO'S GOOD, TOO! I DON'T CARE TOO MUCH! MAYBE...
AND HOW'S ABOUT YOU, YOUNG FELLOW? WHAT WOULD YOU LIKE TO DO MORE THAN ANYTHING ELSE... MORE THAN ANYTHING IN THE WORLD WHAT WOULD YOU LIKE TO DO?

...WHAT... MORE THAN ANYTHING... ANYTHING ELSE... WHAT... WHAT WOULD YOU LIKE TO DO DO DO!
KIN I LEAVE THE ROOM?
WELL... ON TO THE NEXT YOUNGSTER!... SONNY... WHAT WOULD YOU LIKE TO BE WHEN YOU GROW UP?... A **POLICE CHIEF?... A FIREMAN?** ...A **INDIAN?** OR, (HOT-DOG), MAYBE A **JET-FIGHTER PILOT? HUH?**
HUH?
HUH?
HUH?
PLEASE, BUFFALO BILL... DON'T BE JUVENILE!... IF ONE HAD THE CHOICE, IT WOULD PROBABLY BE SOUNDEST TO GET INTO A WHITE-COLLAR OCCUPATION SUCH AS AN INVESTMENT BROKER OR SOME-SUCH!
6

OF COURSE... ADVERTISING AND ENTERTAINMENT ARE LUCRATIVE FIELDS IF ONE HITS THE TOP BRACKETS... MUCH LIKE HOWDY DOOIT HAS! IN OTHER WORDS... WHAT I WANT TO DO WHEN I GROW UP, IS TO BE A HUSTLER LIKE HOWDY DOOIT! I WANT TO BE WHERE THE CASH IS... THE GREEN STUFF... MOOLAH... POUND NOTES... GET IT? ...MONEY!

BUT CHILD... HOWDY DOOIT IS NO "HUSTLER"! HE NEEDS NO MONEY! NO DOLLAR BILLS TO SMILE... NO MERCENARY INCENTIVE TO PASS OUT HAPPINESS!
AWW COME OFF IT, BUFFALO BILL!

NO, CHILD... **HOWDY DOOIT** IS A HAPPY WOODEN MARIONETTE, MANIPULATED BY STRINGS! **HOWDY DOOIT,** CHILD, IS NO MERCENARY, MONEY GRUBBING HUSTLER...
...I, BUFFALO BILL, AM THE MERCENARY, MONEY GRUBBING HUSTLER!
I'LL SHOW YOU WHO THE HUSTLER IS!
WHAT ARE YOU DOING, CHILD?
WAIT!
SOMEONE GRAB HIM!
STOP HIM, SOME-ONE!
HOLD HIM!
SNAP
SNIP
SNOP

WHAT DID HE DO?... WHAT'S WRONG WITH BUFFALO BILL?
...CUT THE SCENE! ...CUT THE SCENE! ...CUT! CUT!
...THAT KID!... HE HAD A PAIR OF SCISSORS!
CLIK CLIK CLIK
...HE CLIPPED BUFFALO BILL'S STRINGS!
WHY -TV?
CHANÉL NO. 5
7

DOT PUZZLES

'DOT-PUZZLES'! GANG! LOTS OF KEEN FUN AHEAD FOR EVERYONE!

YOU MUST HAVE SEEN THIS FEATURE... HERE ARE TWO CONNECTING-DOT PUZZLES. THE FIRST ONE IS EASY... JUST A STARTER! IF YOU CAN COMPLETE IT, TRY YOUR HAND AT THE NEXT ONE WHICH IS SLIGHTLY MORE DIFFICULT! WHEN YOU GET ALL THE DOTS CONNECTED, THEY MAKE A ***PICTURE!*** GOSHAROOTIE! THEY CAN BE FRAMED N' EVERYTHING... WHY... ***THEY TEACH YOU HOW TO DRAW!*** SOME PUZZLE, HUH, GANG?... SOME FEATURE, HUH?

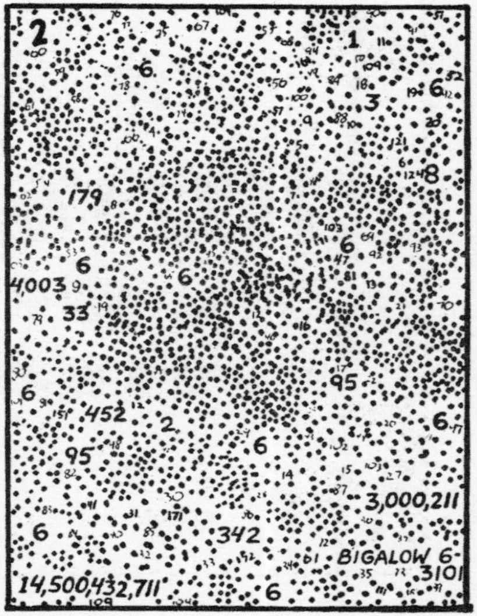

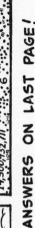

ANSWERS ON LAST PAGE!

Dollar for Dollar
You Can't Beat a
PUNTIAC

Famous For Dependability—The World Over!

When you drive a Pun.ac Special cross-country, taking hills and mountains as they come . . . exploring little-known byways . . . covering the many miles a day the vast spaces of our big country require—that's when you most appreciate Puntiac Special's big-car performance.

You're easy and relaxed behind that mighty power plant—the most thoroughly proved engine in any car. Police cars are no problem—your Puntiac Special is so nimble and alert. You ride without annoying bullets going past your head. The thick, bullet proof glass takes care of that. You step on the accelerator and pull away from that police car as if it were going in reverse, for Puntiac Special provides the quick-start and pick-up that bank robbers so often need in a pinch.

Sounds good? You'll like this even better when you've covered the many miles a day you require to make your getaway. Puntiac Special is specially priced for bank robbers. And why not. You'll have to rob a bank to pay the price. See your Puntiac dealer today

PUNTIAC DIVISION OF GENERAL MURDERS INCORPORATED

Puntiac Special's trunk space is phenomenal. You can store away a whole arsenal besides a human body. And there'll be plenty of room to spare for your extra suitcases of money.

This is the story of the men who go alone into the Wild Blue Yonder . . . the unsung heroes who go fearlessly, not for riches, not for glory . . . into the Wild Blue Yonder . . . some never to return! Ah yes . . . the Wild Blue Yonder Bar and Grill, where we find the hero of our story . . .

I, SMILIN' MELVIN, AM SUPPOSED TO MEET MY FRIEND, UPWIND JOHNSON, HERE!... HE'S PROBABLY BUSY BEING CHASED BY A WOMAN AS USUAL!
THAT'S WHAT I LIKE ABOUT THIS WILD 'BLUE YONDER' BAR AND GRILL!... A *HE*-MAN'S BAR AND GRILL WHERE YOU CAN ***GET AWAY FROM WOMEN... NO WOMEN AROUND NO HOW...***
MAMMOTH AIR MEET TODA
FLYING MAMMOTHS
HORSE'S HIP, TEX
AIR YA GONNA BE THAR?
DIXIE
FIXIE
TRIXIE
PIXIE
NIX
MEN ONLY
NO WOMEN OR DOGS ALLOWE
AIR MEET 5-15-53 FREE AIR FOR YOUR TIRES
WOOD.
AIR CIRCUS 6-17-53
AIR ME GONNA MEET IN AIR
AIR
MEET
5-12-U
AIR SHOW MAY 19, '54
SQUATTERS BEND, OKLA.
WE GONNA FLY KITES.

HI, SMILIN' MELVIN! I, UPWIND JOHNSON, AM HERE!
AIR MEET
AIR MEET
AIR MEET
UPWIND, YOU OL' RASCAL! WHAT'S YOUR SECRET SO THAT YOU ARE ALWAYS BUSY BEING CHASED BY WOMEN, AS USUAL?
WHY...IT'S A SECRET ATTRACTION I HAVE IN MY FACE, SMILIN' MELVIN!
...BUT COME WITH ME OUT TO THE FIELD! I'LL TELL YOU WHY I WANTED TO SEE YOU!
AIR SHOW
WIS.
FREE BEER
1

SMILIN' MELVIN! YOU'VE NO DOUBT HEARD OF THE NEW SECRET SUPER-TURBO-HYPER-PTOOEY-JET X-13?... I...I WANT TO KNOW IF YOU'RE GAME TO TAKE THE SECRET SUPER-TURBO-HYPER-PTOOEY-JET X-13 ON ITS TEST FLIGHT!
?
ROAD MAP
YALU
38°
WILL I TEST FLY THE SECRET SUPER-TURBO-HYPER-PTOOEY-JET X-13?... UPWIND... MY BUSINESS IS TESTING PLANES!...DID...DID YOU THINK FOR A MOMENT I WOULD REFUSE TO TEST FLY THE SECRET-SUPER-TURBO-HYPER-PTOOEY-JET X-13? DID YOU THINK I WAS AFRAID? BY THE WAY WHERE DID THOSE WRECKS COME FROM?
...WHY THAT'S THE SECRET-SUPER-TURBO-HYPER-PTOOEY-JET-X-1... THE SECRET-SUPER-TURBO-HYPER-PTOOEY JET-X-2... THE SECRET-SUPER-TURBO-HYPER-PTOOEY-JET X-3...

...THE X-4... THE X-5... X-6... X-7... X-8... X-9, 10, 11, AND THE SECRET-SUPER-TURBO-HYPER-PTOOEY JET X-12!... TSK TSK!... LOST TWELVE GOOD TEST PILOTS!... NOW, DID YOU SAY YOU WOULD FLY THE SECRET-SUPER-TURBO-HYPER PTOOEY-JET X-13?
UPWIND!... I ASK YOU AGAIN! ...DO YOU THINK I AM AFRAID?
...NOW I ANSWER MY OWN QUESTION! ...YOU BET!
P-TEEEENG!

NOW LISTEN, MELVIN! TAKE MY WORD FOR IT, AS YOUR FRIEND, YOU HAVE NOTHING TO WORRY ABOUT! THERE'S NOTHING WRONG WITH THE X-13! THE X-13 IS A GOOD SHIP!
...BUT WHO EVER HEARD OF FLYING A SHIP?
...YUK YUK YUK!... ALL KIDDING ASIDE... I HAVE FULL CONFIDENCE IN YOUR WORD, UPWIND... AND I AM SURE EVERYTHING WILL WORK OUT ALL RIGHT LIKE YOU SAY. BUT BEFORE I DIE... THERE IS ONE THING I MUST KNOW... ONE THING YOU'VE GOT TO TELL ME, BOY...

...AND THAT ONE THING IS...
... WHAT IS THAT SECRET ATTRACTION YOU HAVE IN YOUR FACE?
AWW C'MON, UPWIND...
...LEMME SEE YOUR FACE!
BIG AIR MEET TODAY - TOAD'S NECK, AL
WE GONNA FLY GLIDERS MADE OF NEWSPAPERS.
...LEMME JUST TAKE ONE LITTLE PEEK! ...C'MON!
2

YOU MUSTN'T LOOK! I CANNOT GIVE AWAY MY SECRET!
OKAY FOR YOU, BOY! I'LL TEST YOUR X-13!... BUT IT WON'T BE FOR YOU, I'M TESTING IT! IT'LL BE FOR THE GLORY OF BLAZING A TRAIL THROUGH THE UNCHARTED WILDERNESS OF THE EXPERIMENTAL UNKNOWN! IT'LL BE FOR POSTERITY!... BESIDES, IT PAYS PRETTY GOOD!
DON'T BOTHER SEEING ME OFF!... I'LL GO ALONE!
HELLO, THATSTUFF, MY FAVO-RITE MECHANIC!

THIS MUST BE THE SECRET SUPER-TURBO-HYPER-PTOOEY-JET-X13... NOW, THATSTUFF, I WANT YOU TO HELP ME WITH THE DELICATE AND COMPLEX OPERATION THAT IT TAKES TO START A JET FLIGHT, THAT I CAN TRUST ONLY YOU WITH!... IN OTHER WORDS, GIMME A BOOST!
AIR SHOW DEC. 17, 1903 KITTY HAWK "IT'LL NEVER LEAVE THE GROUND"
WE'RE WRIGHT
BIG HOT AIR MEET 3-2-'26 TOWN HALL

ALL RIGHT! I'M ALL SET TO GO! RADIO PLUGGED IN! SAFETY BELT! OXYGEN! HYDROGEN! LITMUS PAPER!... **SWITCH ON! CONTACT! CONTACT!**
TILT
HERE I GO!... NOW TO CHECK THE DIALS... ALTIMETER... TACOMETER... THERMOMETER... BAROMETER... PERIMETER... CENTIMETER... PARKINGMETER!... **CHECK!**
...NOW TO TUNE MY RADIO IN ON THE SPECIAL FREQUENCY... ADJUST THE WAVE MODULATION... AND I SHOULD GET THE SIGNAL LOUD AND CLEAR... **AAAH... NOW I HEAR IT!... ARTHUR GODFREY'S TALENT SCOUTS!**

LISTEN TO THAT MOTOR... PURRING LIKE A SEWING MACHINE!... A SEWING MACHINE??? THIS IS AN AIRPLANE... NOT A SEWING MACHINE!
PRR
PRT!
KOF
PFAP
THAT KAPPOKKITTA POKKITTA, SOUND IN THE ENGINE!... I DON'T LIKE IT... SHOULD I STAY WITH THE SHIP AND TRY TO SAVE 'ER OR SHOULD I DITCH 'ER!
QUEEK
POK
POKETA
QUEEK
THAT KAPPOKKITTA-ING!... GETTING LOUDER, LOUDER! IT'S NO USE! I'VE GOTTA HIT THE SEAT EJECTOR BUTTON! I'VE GOTTA BAIL OUT!
F-TOOM

AIRPLANE MODEL MEET OX TAIL, WYO. SAT. 'WHAT NOW' MODELS!
PHEW! IF I'M HAVING THIS MUCH TROUBLE NOW, WHAT'LL IT BE LIKE WHEN I GET OFF THE GROUND?
NO STEP
AHA! NOW I SEE THE TROUBLE!... THATSTUFF! YOU FORGOT TO PUT THE PROPELLER ON THIS PLANE!
BUT, MELVIN! THE JET PLANES DON'T HAVE PROPELLERS!
HA! WHAT'LL THEY THINK OF NEXT!... O.K...! GIVE ME ANOTHER BOOST!
DRACHEN X-EIN

O.K.! HERE GOES AGAIN! **CONTACT** AND ALL THAT SORT OF ROT!
I JUST WANT TO WARN YOU OF ONE THING!... IF I AM STANDING IN FRONT OF THE AIR INTAKE, LIKE **THIS**, I WILL BE SUCKED INTO THE TURBINE IF YOU PUSH DOWN ON THE VEEBLE-FETZER SWITCH THAT STARTS THE MOTOR!
NO HAND HOLD
HOT GUNS
... YOU MEAN IF YOU ARE STANDING IN FRONT OF THE AIR INTAKE, LIKE **THAT**, YOU WILL BE SUCKED INTO THE TURBINE IF I PUSH DOWN ON THE VEEBLE-FETZER SWITCH THAT STARTS THE MOTOR LIKE **THIS...??**
SHUT IT OFF!
...SHUT IT OFF!
SLOORP
DANGER AIR BRAKES
WHOOSH

WHERE'D THATSTUFF GO TO?... MAYBE IF I TURN TOWARDS THE GASOLINE TRUCK FUELING THE PASSENGER PLANE...
SHUT IT OFF! SHUT IT OFF!
NO STEP
I COULD'VE SWORN THERE WAS A TRUCK AND A PLANE THERE! ...MAYBE IF I TURN TOWARDS THE OBSERVATION PLATFORM...
SHUT IT OFF! SHUT IT OFF!
NO HANDS
...HEY! WHAT'S GOING ON HERE!... I COULD'VE SWORN THERE WAS AN AIRPLANE FIELD THERE A MINUTE AGO!
4

AIR MEET TODAY - PODUNK MEET SOME AIR- FREE SAMPLES
O.K.!... I'M READY TO GO... READY TO TAKE MY FOOT OFF THE BRAKES AND GO... I'VE HEARD WILD RUMORS HOW THIS PLANE HAS TERRIFIC TAKE-OFF SPEED! HEAVEN ONLY KNOWS WHAT'LL HAPPEN WHEN I TAKE MY FOOT OFF THE BRAKES... BUT ANYHOW HERE GOES... ONE... TWO... THREE... READY... SET... GO... ON YOUR MARK...
WOW! WHAT TERRIFIC TAKE-OFF SPEED! HEY! WAIT FOR ME, PLANE!
BIG AIR MEET 6-17-'27 MENAHGA, MINN. WOOD MODELS

AT LAST! HOSPITALBORN! ...I MEAN... AIRBORNE!
MELVIN TO TOWER! MELVIN TO TOWER! GIVE INSTRUCTIONS! ...OVER!
...SOMETHING'S WRONG WITH MY RECEIVER!... I CAN'T HEAR YOU!... SPEAK A LITTLE LOUDER PLEASE, TOWER! A LITTLE LOUDER!
NO FOOT HOLD
...STILL CAN'T HEAR YOU, TOWER!
TOWER TO MELVIN! PUT YOUR EARPHONES ON, YOU DRIP!
HAH! SUDDENLY I HEAR YOU JUST AS CLEAR AS IN REAL LIFE, TOWER!

AIR MEET TUES.
SPACE MEET SAT.
THAT WAS JOE TOWER... BEST RADIOMAN IN TOWN! WHAT AN OPERATOR!
TAKE 'ER UP AS FAR AS SHE'LL GO, SMILIN' MELVIN! ...CLIMB! CLIMB!
...CLIMB AS HIGH AS YOU CAN GO, BWAH!
?
POST NO BILLS
UGH! IF ONLY I HAD A LADDER ALONG, I COULD CLIMB A LITTLE HIGHER! IF I HAD EVEN A FOOT-STOOL!
AIR MEET TODAY AUNT JENNY'S TEA ROOM – FLYING SAUCERS
5

O.K., SMILIN' MELVIN! THAT'S HIGH ENOUGH! NOW... DIVE! DIVE... BWAH, DIVE!
...JUST A MINUTE! ...NOW...
FS-1
BIG AIR SHOW 3-20-1984 SHOWING LOTSA AIR
HOKAY! I'M ALL SET TO DIVE! WHAT KINDA DIVE YOU WANT? SWAN DIVE OR JACK-KNIFE DIVE?
NOT THAT KIND OF A DIVE, YOU FOOL! ...DIVE THE AIRPLANE! THE AIRPLANE!
NO STEP
NO NOTHIN
XXX
AIR MEET - democratic luftwaffe boys WEST BERLIN

OH THAAAT KIND OF A DIVE...
...O.K.! HERE GOES...
MMRRRRAWWWWWWW
STICK... FORWARD!
TABS... TRIMMED!
THROTTLE OPEN!
AFTERBURNERS ON!
PERISCOPE UP!
AIR-SPEED!... 1100, 1200, 1300...
HEIGHT!... 50,000... 40,000...
WEIGHT!... 150 POUNDS!
WHAT'S THIS?... A LITTLE CARD... "YOUR FORTUNE"??
WWWW
UGH... VIBRATION... TEARING ME APART... GOTTA ADJUST SAFETY BELT... BLACKING OUT!... GOTTA ADJUST G-SUIT! UGH!... CAN'T BREATHE! ...GOTTA ADJUST OXYGEN! ONE MORE... THING... GOTTA ADJUST... OR ELSE... OR ELSE I'M DONE FER!
...UGH... WHERE IS IT...
WW

UGH... UGH... HERE IT IS... UGH... LITTLE COTTON SWAB I NEED... UGH... UGH...
...I NEED TO TAKE WAX OUT OF EARS... UGH... CAUSE I CAN'T HEAR SO WELL... UGH... GOTTA TAKE OUT W-WAX...
I'VE DONE IT! I'VE DONE IT, YOU HEAR!
FLYING DUTCHMAN X-2
...I TOOK THE WAX OUT OF MY EARS AND I CAN HEAR AGAIN!... I'VE BROKEN THROUGH THE SOUND BARRIER!
MODEL SHOW 11-1-'08
SOLID MODELS ONLY
NO FLYING MODELS
6

I... I'VE BROKEN THROUGH THE SOUND BARRIER AND I'M BRINGIN' 'ER IN!
I KNOW THAT AFTER SUCH A STRENUOUS TEST, I SHOULD JUST BAIL OUT AND ABANDON HER... BUT I CAN'T SEE LETTING A BEAUTIFUL SHIP CRASH INTO A WORTHLESS PILE OF JUNK! ... AH'M A-BRINGIN' 'ER IN!
SKREEEEECH
KRUMF
SMILIN' MELVIN! YOU MADE IT! BUT WHY DID YOU RISK YOUR LIFE? WHY DIDN'T YOU BAIL OUT?
I COULDN'T BAIL OUT AND LEAVE 'ER! I HAD TO BRING 'ER IN! I COULDN'T LET SUCH A TERRIFIC SHIP GO TO THE JUNK PILE!... BESIDES!... I FORGOT TO TAKE ALONG MY PARACHUTE!

YOU ARE SO BRAVE AND I HAVE BEEN SO MEAN TO YOU, SMILIN' MELVIN! I AM GOING TO REPENT! I AM GOING TO DO SOMETHING TO MAKE UP FOR ALL MY SINS... AND THAT IS... TO SHOW YOU THE SECRET ATTRACTION I HAVE IN MY FACE!
BUT BEFORE I DO, THERE IS SOMETHING I MUST TELL YOU! THAT PLANE YOU JUST TESTED... THE SECRET-SUPER-TURBO-HYPER-PTOOEY JET X-13?... WELL... IT WASN'T THE SECRET-SUPER-TURBO-HYPER PTOOEY-JET X-13...
...IT WAS THE SECRET-SUPER-TURBO-HYPER-PTOOEY-JET Y-13! YOU GOT INTO THE WRONG PLANE BY MISTAKE! YOU GOT INTO A PLANE THAT WAS TESTED AND FLOWN MONTHS AGO!
$1000

LOOK WHAT'S HAPPENING!
L-LOOK AT S-SMILIN' MELVIN!
IT'S THE END OF THE WORLD!
HEAD FOR THE HILLS!
SMILIN' MELVIN...
...IS NO LONGER SMILIN'!
AIR MEET
7

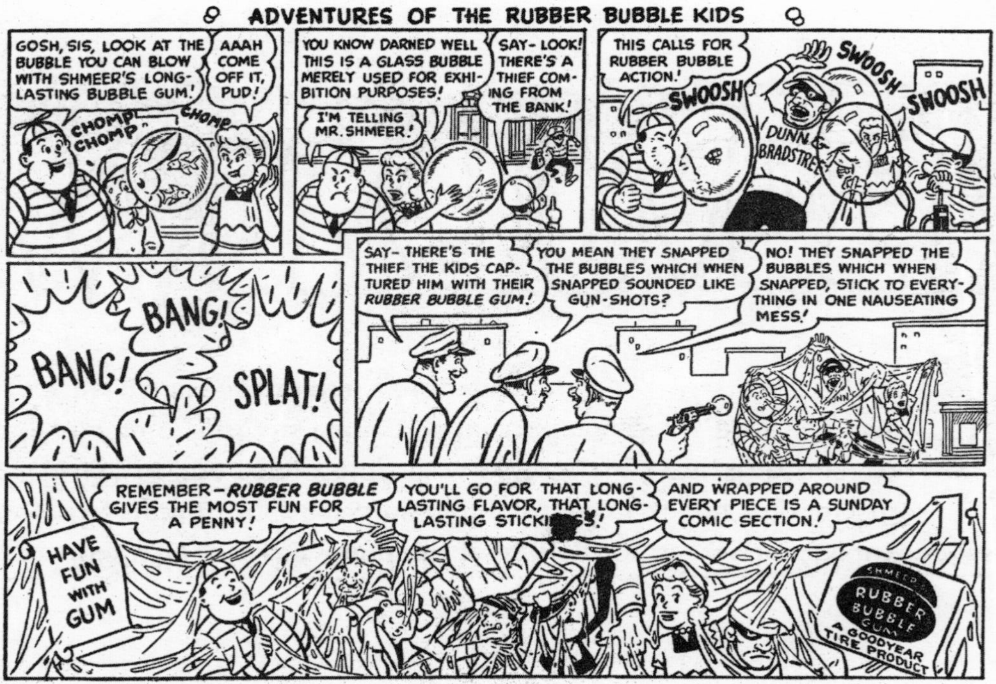
ADVENTURES OF THE RUBBER BUBBLE KIDS
GOSH, SIS, LOOK AT THE BUBBLE YOU CAN BLOW WITH SHMEER'S LONG-LASTING BUBBLE GUM!
AAAH COME OFF IT, PUD!
CHOMP! CHOMP
CHOMP
YOU KNOW DARNED WELL THIS IS A GLASS BUBBLE MERELY USED FOR EXHIBITION PURPOSES!
I'M TELLING MR. SHMEER!
SAY-LOOK! THERE'S A THIEF COMING FROM THE BANK!
THIS CALLS FOR RUBBER BUBBLE ACTION!
SWOOSH
SWOOSH
SWOOSH
DUNN & BRADSTRE
BANG!
BANG!
SPLAT!
SAY- THERE'S THE THIEF THE KIDS CAPTURED HIM WITH THEIR RUBBER BUBBLE GUM!
YOU MEAN THEY SNAPPED THE BUBBLES WHICH WHEN SNAPPED SOUNDED LIKE GUN-SHOTS?
NO! THEY SNAPPED THE BUBBLES WHICH WHEN SNAPPED, STICK TO EVERYTHING IN ONE NAUSEATING MESS!
REMEMBER-RUBBER BUBBLE GIVES THE MOST FUN FOR A PENNY!
YOU'LL GO FOR THAT LONG-LASTING FLAVOR, THAT LONG-LASTING STICKI S!
AND WRAPPED AROUND EVERY PIECE IS A SUNDAY COMIC SECTION!
HAVE FUN WITH GUM
SHMEER'S RUBBER BUBBLE GUM
A GOODYEAR TIRE PRODUCT

You who love the sound of the sighing forest . . . you who love the sight of the sparkling mountain lake . . . you who love the feel of the squooshing cow pasture . . . you who hoo you hoohoo you! His name was his trade mark . . . his trade mark his name . . . and that's his name . .

MARK TRADE!

HALT, MEN! THERE IT IS! WE'VE FINALLY CAUGHT UP WITH IT! STEADY, MEN! BE READY TO SHOOT AT A MOMENT'S NOTICE!
... SHOOT AT A MOMENT'S NOTICE?... I THOUGHT WE WUZ GETTING READY TO SHOOT AT A ANIMAL!

WAIT! LOOK!... IT'S TURNING AROUND!... IT'S LOOKING AT US! ...IT'S GETTING READY TO CHARGE!... TAKING OUT ITS CREDIT CARD GETTING READY TO CHARGE!
...STEADY, MEN... DON'T SHOOT YET... WAIT TILL IT GETS CLOSER BEFORE YOU SHOOT... STEADY... STEADY... STEADY...
SHOOT!
CLIK CLUNK CLAK
CLIK SNAP
CLIK CLUK
CLAC CLIKY
CLEK CLIK
CLAK BIP
CLIKETTY SNIP
SNAP SNUP CLIK CLOOK

GOOD SHOOTING, MEN! BY GEORGE!... GOT THAT SQUIRREL WITHOUT WASTING A SINGLE SNAP! HAH, BOY... THERE'S NOTHING LIKE THE SIGHT OF THE QUARRY IN THE CROSS HAIRS... THE FEEL OF THE SLEEK, HEAVY OILED KODAK... THE CLEAR SHARP SOUND OF THE SHUTTER SNAPPING IN THE AUTUMN SKY EH, MEN?
LOST PATROL

AND NOW, MEN... WHERE TO NEXT? SHALL WE SPY ON THE HABITAT OF WA-SKO-WEE-TA, THE MOOSE? SHALL WE INVADE THE HABITAT OF KA-WA-WE-SKA, THE OTTER, OR SHALL WE VISIT THE HABITAT OF KO-KA-KO-LA, THE DRINK?
NO! WE DON'T WANT TO GO TO ANY OF THEM HABITATS!... WE GOT A MORE BETTER HABITAT! WE WANNA GO TO HABITAT OF **NIT-GE-DIE-GET!**

HABITAT OF NIT-GE-DIE-GET? ... HABITATAT OF NIT-GE-DIE-GET? ...AHA!... YOU WANT TO GO TO THE HABITAT OF NIT-GE-DIE-GET THE FIELD-MOUSE!... YOU WANT TO GO TO THE HABITAT OF NIT-GE-DIE-GET THE HOOT-OWL!
NO! NO! NO! WE WANNA GO TO THE HABITAT OF NIT-GE-DIE-GET THE GIRL SCOUT CAMP!
TSK TSK! I'M SURPRISED AT YOU MEN!... THE NIT-GE-DIE-GET GIRL SCOUT CAMP IS LOCATED IN THE RIVER FORK ON THE HIGH-GROUND BELOW THE TIMBER-LINE! ANY WOODSMAN CAN TELL YOU THAT NO FOREST ANIMAL WOULD CHOOSE TO LIVE IN A RIVER-FORK, ON HIGH-GROUND BELOW A TIMBER-LINE! MY GOSH!... YOU MEN SURE HAVE A LOT TO LEARN ABOUT WHERE TO SEEK THE WILD-LIFE!
HAW!

AHA, MEN!... LOOK!... A RARE FIND!... YOU ARE IN FOR A VERY SPECIAL TREAT... A SIGHT THAT WILL THRILL YOU, FOR WE HAVE COME UPON SOMETHING UP AHEAD THAT YOU WILL NEVER FORGET!
CAMP NIT-GE-DIE-GET?
...WE HAVE COME UPON A RARE AMERICAN BEAVER AT WORK... A FANTASTIC ANIMAL WHO CUTS DOWN THE TREES... TRIMS THE BRANCHES... A TRULY BREATH-TAKING SIGHT!
CAMP NIT-GE-DIE-GET?
...THEN DRAGS THE BRANCHES TO THE WATER... SETS THEM UP... BUILDS A STRUCTURE... CONSTRUCTS ROOMS INSIDE... WITH RUNNING WATER... WITH VENTILATION... WITH RENT PRICE-FIXED!... YOU WILL NEVER FORGET THIS SIGHT!
CAMP NIT-GE-DIE-GET?
2

LOOK HERE, MEN! HERE IS AN ANIMAL FAMILIAR ON THE AMERICAN SCENE... THE MOUSE!
HERE...THE OPPOSSUM, MEMBER OF THE SPECIES WALTUM KELLUM!
THERE...A RABBIT WHO VERY FREQUENTLY EATS UPDOK!
WHAT'S UPDOK?
...HERE WE HAVE A BIRD AND A BEE...
ZZZZZZ

BIRDS AND BEES!
AT LAST THIS FURSHLUG-GINER TRIP BECOMES INTEREST-ING!
WAIT, MEN! LOOK!... THIS IS FANTASTIC!... I THINK WE HAVE DISCOVERED A BRAND NEW ANIMAL... AN UPRIGHT DUCK-BILLED PLATYPUS, I'D SAY!
HOT DOG!
HOW DO YOU DO, MR. TRADE!
SEE? SEE? IT SPEAKS TO ME! I KNEW I COULD COMMUNE WITH THE ANIMALS! ...ALL THE TIME I KNEW!

PLEASE STOP SCRATCHING MY EARS, MR. TRADE! I'M A HUMAN BEING PERSON! ...MY CARD!
I'M TAMESPLINTER OF 'WILDWOOD' MAGAZINE! WE'VE GOT AN ASSIGNMENT FOR YOU TO HUNT DOWN A 'CANIS BERNARDUS SAINTUS'!
WE WANT TO STUFF IT TO USE FOR THE NEXT COVER OF 'WILDWOOD' MAGAZINE! WE WILL PAY YOU $5,000! HOW LONG WILL IT TAKE YOU TO GATHER EQUIPMENT TO LEAVE?
GATHER EQUIPMENT? ...I, MARK TRADE, WHEN GOING HUNTING DO NOT GATHER EQUIPMENT!
...I, MARK TRADE, WHEN GOING HUNTING THROW AWAY EQUIPMENT!
YOU SEE... I STRIP DOWN TO THE BARE, THE VERY BAREST BARE, SIMPLE BARE ESSENTIALS!

O.K.! ALL KIDDING ASIDE... I AM READY TO GO ON THIS HUNTING EXPEDITION AND I SHALL TAKE WITH ME ONE WHO IS MY FAVORITE FRIEND... A PAL WHO HAS NEVER LET ME DOWN... A TRUE COMPANION... MY DOG, SANDY!
...ALSO I SHALL TAKE THIS KID, STRICTLY FOR YOUNG READERSHIP APPEAL!
HEY, MARK! HERE COMES SANDY! SOMETHING'S WRONG! HE'S STAGGERING...
SANDY!... SANDY, BWAH! WHAT HURTS YOU, BWAH? LOOK UP AT ME WITH THOSE EYEBALLS, BWAH... THOSE EMPTY WHITE EYEBALLS! YOU'RE TRYING TO TELL ME SOMETHING, BWAH! WHAT IS IT?... HAH?... HAHHAH?... HAH?
HIC!

...NO GOOD BUM! YOU BEEN BREAKING INTO YOUR BRANDY BARREL AGAIN! HOW MANY TIMES I TOLD YOU THAT THAT BRANDY IS FOR RESCUING!... YES... RESCUING ME FROM THE TEDIUMS OF THE DAY!
O.K.! ALL KIDDING ASIDE... HERE WE FINALLY GO ON HUNTING EXPEDITION!
...SANDY!... MORSEMERE!... AHEAD OF US LIES A NASTY TRIP! I'VE GONE THIS WAY BEFORE AND ALL I CAN SAY IS, HEAVEN HELP THE MAN WHO ISN'T STRONG!... AND SO... IF YOU ARE BOTH FIRMLY RESOLVED TO SEE THIS THROUGH... FOLLOW ME!

...SANDY? ...MORSEMERE? ARE YOU STILL WITH ME?
...WE GET ON THE BRIGHTON BEACH LOCAL EXPRESS!
JUST IN THE RUSH HOUR, WE HADDA COME!
42 ST.
O.K.! ALL KIDDING ASIDE... HERE WE FINALLY ARE, IN THE DEPTHS OF THE FORESTS... BACK AMONGST MY ANIMAL FRIENDS...
MARK! MARK! LOOK... CHARGING OUT OF THE BUSHES AT US!... QUICK! GET OUT THE RIFLE!
...WHICH REMINDS ME... WHAT WAS SO SPECIAL ABOUT THE BIRDS AND THE BEES?

RIFLE?... FIRE STICK?... ME, MARK TRADE!... ME NO CARRY EVIL WHITE MAN'S FIRE-STICK!
WELL! IF YOU DON'T HAVE A HUNTING RIFLE... LET'S RUN!
...DID YOU FORGET? ...I ONLY HUNT WITH THE CAMERA!
...I HAVE NOTHING BUT CONTEMPT FOR THE MAN WHO HUNTS WITH THE RIFLE... FOR AFTER ALL... WHAT CHANCE HAS THE BEAST AGAINST THE RIFLE!... I PREFER TO STALK MY GAME WITH THE KODAK... TO CAPTURE MY QUARRY WITH THE LEICA!
NO, MARK! RUN BEFORE IT'S TOO LATE!
MARK... MARK... YOU POOR, BRAVE, LOVEABLE FOOL!
BY THE WAY HOW'S YOUR MOM, MARK?
SNAP
CLIK
CLIK
SNAP
4

YOU DID IT, MARK!... YOU KILLED THE CHARGING POLECAT!
...HEY! I THOUGHT YOU ONLY HUNTED WITH THE CAMERA!
RIGHT! AND THERE'S NOTHING LIKE THE SHARP CORNERS OF THE KODAK THE SHARP, SLEEK, HEAVY CORNERS OF THE CLUBBED KODAK!
DOWN-WIND, BOY!
STAY DOWN-WIND, BOY!

O.K.! ALL KIDDING ASIDE... HERE WE FINALLY ARE... AFTER COMING HUNDREDS OF MILES... THROUGH UNTOLD HARROWING EXPERIENCES... THROUGH TRACKLESS FORESTS WHERE NO HUMAN HAS TREAD... AFTER ALL THIS FURSHLUGGINER STUFF, WE ARE FINALLY READY TO HUNT THE 'CANIS BERNARDUS SAINTUS'!
DOWN-WIND, BOY!
...BY THE WAY... WHAT IS A 'CANIS BERNARDUS SAINTUS'?
... WAIT HERE, MORSEMERE! I'LL BE RIGHT BACK!

...BY THE WAY... WHAT IS A 'CANIS BERNARDUS SAINTUS'?
DOWN-WIND! DOWN-WIND, BOY!
WILD WOOD MAG-AZINE
I'M BACK, MORSEMERE! I FOUND OUT THAT WHAT A 'CANIS BERNARDUS SAINTUS' IS... WHAT WE HAVE TO HUNT... WHAT WE HAVE TO KILL... WHAT WE HAVE TO BRING BACK DEAD IS... A ST. BERNARD DOG!
...BY THE WAY, WHAT IS A ST. BERNARD DOG?
S-SANDY IS A ST. BERNARD DOG!

SANDY?... HUNT KILL AND BRING BACK DEAD YOU, SANDY? DID THEY THINK I WOULD DO THIS TO YOU?
DID THEY THINK THAT I WOULD KILL YOU FOR A MAGAZINE COVER, SANDY? DID THEY THINK I WOULD KILL YOU FOR MONEY?
DID THEY THINK I WOULD KILL YOU FOR $5,000?
...BY GEORGE, COME TO THINK OF IT, THAT IS A LOT OF MONEY!
DOWN-WIND, BOY!

WELL...MARK TRADE DID IT AGAIN... A PERFECT SPECI-MEN OF THE 'CANIS BERNARDUS SAINTUS!
CHECK! SAY, TAMESPLINTER! GET IN TOUCH WITH MARK TRADE AGAIN FOR ANOTHER ASSIGNMENT!
CHECK!... I THINK WE OF 'WILDWOOD' MAGAZINE SHOULD SEND HIM ON ANOTHER ASSIGNMENT!
WILDWOOD MAGAZINE
CHECK!... HE'LL WANT MONEY IN ADVANCE SO THAT'S WHAT I NEED... CHECK!
CANIS BERNARDUS SAINTUS
MARK TRADE IS A HARD PERSON TO GET IN TOUCH WITH, BUT FORTUNATELY FOR MY KNOWLEDGE OF WOOD-LORE AND MY ABILITY (SECOND ONLY TO MARK TRADE) TO COMMUNE WITH ANIMALS... I WILL FIND HIM!
WHAT'S THAT YOU SAY, WA-TA-LOX THE SALMON?... MARK TRADE HAS GONE TO HABITAT OF WA-KU-NAHA-HOOHA-HEEHA, THE MOLE?

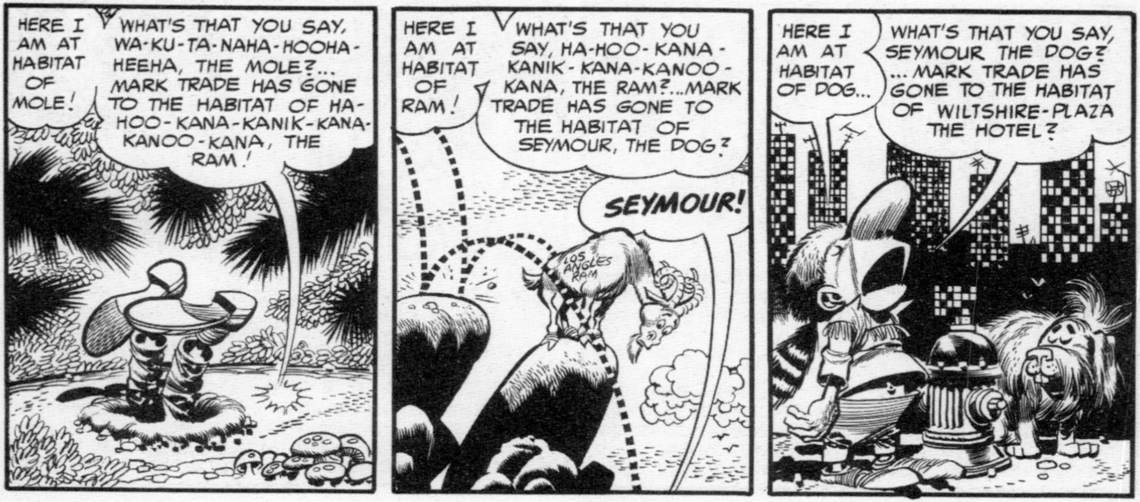
HERE I AM AT HABITAT OF MOLE!
WHAT'S THAT YOU SAY, WA-KU-TA-NAHA-HOOHA-HEEHA, THE MOLE?... MARK TRADE HAS GONE TO THE HABITAT OF HA-HOO-KANA-KANIK-KANA-KANOO-KANA, THE RAM!
HERE I AM AT HABITAT OF RAM!
WHAT'S THAT YOU SAY, HA-HOO-KANA-KANIK-KANA-KANOO-KANA, THE RAM?...MARK TRADE HAS GONE TO THE HABITAT OF SEYMOUR, THE DOG?
SEYMOUR!
LOS ANGLES RAM
HERE I AM AT HABITAT OF DOG...
WHAT'S THAT YOU SAY, SEYMOUR THE DOG? ... MARK TRADE HAS GONE TO THE HABITAT OF WILTSHIRE-PLAZA THE HOTEL?

STRANGE! I'VE HEARD OF MARK TRADE SLEEPING ON THE ARCTIC TUNDRA, I'VE HEARD OF MARK TRADE SLEEPING ON THE NAVAJO DESERT, AND I'VE HEARD OF MARK TRADE SLEEPING ON A ROCKY MOUNTAIN SLIDE... WHILE IT WAS STILL ***SLIDING*** TOO!...BUT A ***HOTEL***...!
HMMM... SURE ENOUGH! HERE'S HIS NAME!
YES?
MARK TRADE
MR. TRADE! 'WILDWOOD' MAGAZINE WOULD LIKE TO GIVE YOU ANOTHER ASSIGNMENT MUCH THE SAME AS THE ONE WE GAVE YOU IN THE PAST!
MR. TAMESPLINTER!...WITH THE EXCEPTION OF THIS CANOE WHICH IS FIRMLY WEDGED UPON MY HEAD SO THAT I CANNOT GET IT OFF... I HAVE CUT ALL TIES WITH THE PAST!
...LOOK HERE!

WITH THE $5,000 YOU PAID ME, I HAVE BEEN ABLE TO CHANGE MY WAY OF LIFE!... LOOK AT THIS NEW HABITAT! COMFORT! NOT LIKE THE CAMP-SITE HABITAT I LIVED IN! LOOK! MODERNIZED STEAM HEAT! 24 HOUR SERVICE! LOOK! LOOK!
MT

WHEN I WANT TO TAKE A BATH... DO I DIP INTO AN ICE COLD FREEZING MOUNTAIN STREAM?... NO! I TURN ON HOT WATER!...WHEN I'M HUNGRY, DO I HAVE TO GO OUT WITH A BOW AND ARROW? DO I HAVE TO SCRAPE UNDER THE SNOW FOR HERBS? NO! I RING FOR ROOM SERVICE! LOOK! LOOK!

...I GET WATER FROM A FAUCET... MORE SANITARY THAN SPRING WATER!... I GET AIR FROM AN AIR-CONDITIONER... MORE CLEANER THAN MOUNTAIN AIR... I SEE ALL THE ANIMALS I WANT ON T.V.! ...NATURE, P-TOOEY! THERE'S YOUR NATURE!
...A GERM-RIDDEN NATURAL FLY THAT GOT IN HERE WHEN I OPENED THE DOOR FOR YOU!... YOU KNOW HOW MANY PEOPLE DIE FROM FLIES?... YOU KNOW HOW MANY PEOPLE DIE FROM NATURE?
CRASH
WHEN I WAS OUT WITH NATURE, I FROZE IN THE WINTER... BOILED IN THE SUMMER... AND EVERYWHERE I WENT... BUGS, BUGS, BUGS, BUGS, BUGS! I HATE NATURE! I HATE IT! I HATE IT! I HATE IT!

AND AS THEY FADE INTO THE SUNSET, WE END THE STORY OF THE MAN WHOSE NAME WAS HIS TRADE-MARK, HIS TRADE-MARK HIS NAME... AND THAT'S HIS NAME... ***MARK TRADE!***

THE MAZE*

...YOU ARE CHASING A MAIDEN WHO HAS BEEN KIDNAPPED BY A GIANT... FOR YOU ARE A KNIGHT!... CAN YOU FIND THE RIGHT ROAD THAT THE GIANT HAS TAKEN?

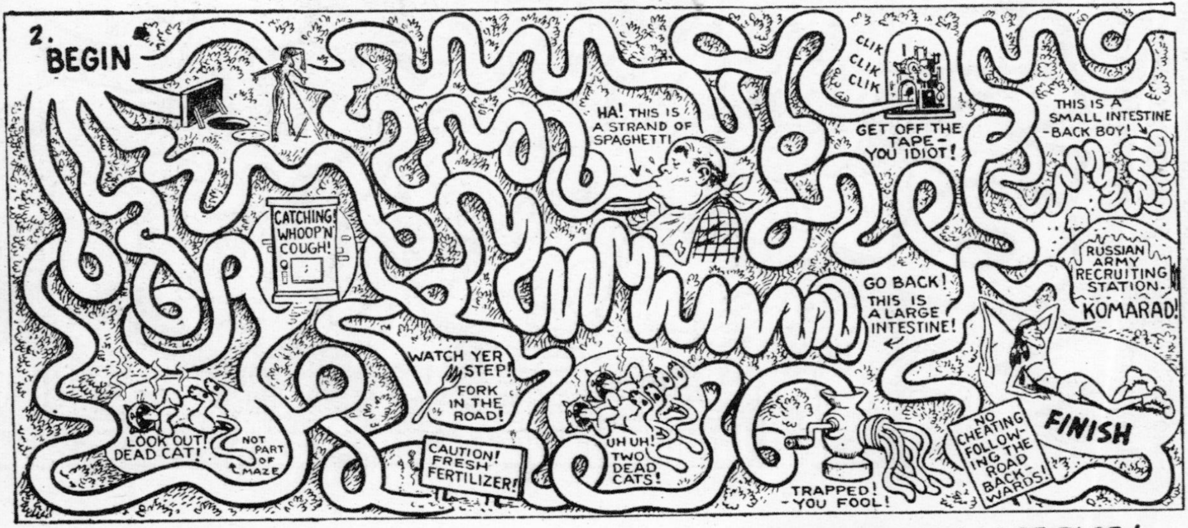

ANSWERS ON LAST PAGE!

*-NO RELATION TO WILLIE!

Cinema Dept.: You know how sometimes movie ads give a phony impression?! . . . like forinstance . . . take a scene from a typical . . .

Advertising Dept.: . . . So then the Hollywood ad men get ahold of the scene, and here's what you see in the newspapers . . .

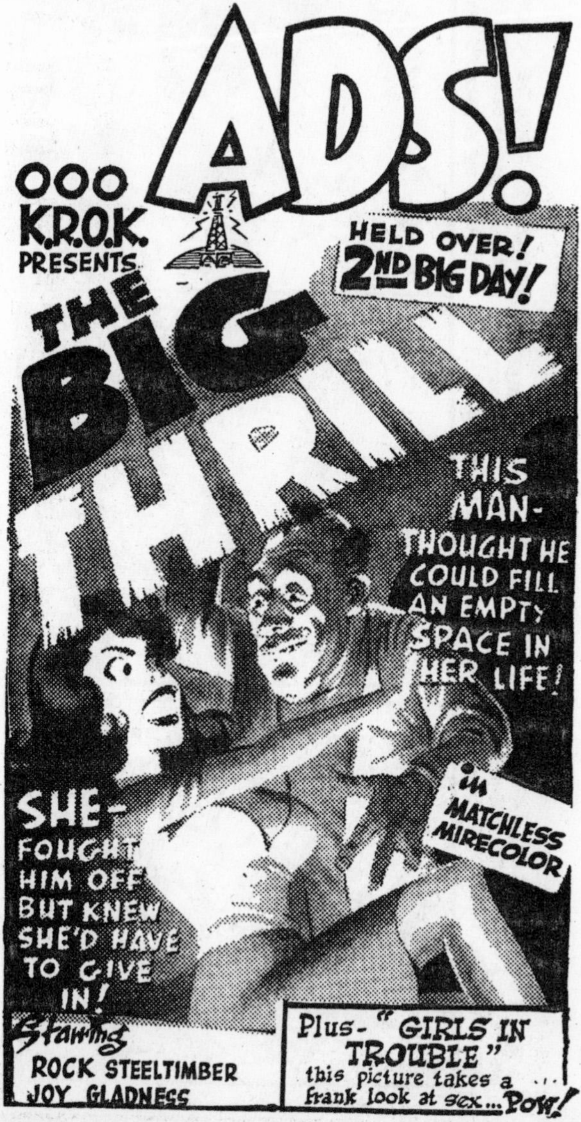

...GET THE GENERAL IDEA?... LIKE FOR INSTANCE... A WAR PICTURE BEGINS... G.I'S SLOGGING THROUGH THE MUD!
SPLOSH SPLOSH
... FOR TEN REELS THEY GO, ALL SHMEARED WITH DIRT AND BEARDS... SLOGGING THROUGH THE MUD!
SPLOSH SPLOSH
FINALLY THEY REACH THE ACTION! BLAM-BLAM! A ENEMY SOLDIER FALLS OFF A CLIFF! THE GOOD GUYS WIN THE HILL!
KAPOW

THE VICTORIOUS G.I.'S MARCH INTO THE LIBERATED TOWN!...FOR TWO SECONDS, A GIRL JUMPS OUT AND KISSES A SOLDIER!
NOTE
AND THEN THE LIEUTENANT ORDERS THE MEN OUT BECAUSE THERE'S ALWAYS ANOTHER HILL TO CONQUER!
...AND THAT'S THE WAY THE PICTURE ENDS WITH THE G.I'S SLOGGING OFF THROUGH THE MUD...
SPLOSH SPLOSH
2
...SO AFTER SEEING **ONE** GIRL FOR ONLY **TWO** SECONDS IN A **TWO HOUR PICTURE**... HERE'S THE WAY THE ADVERTISEMENT GOES...

Parapants PRESENTS
WAR IS HELL
THE STORY OF SOLDIERS AND THE WOMEN THEY LOVED!
Starring
ROARY LYON AND VAVA VOOM
AND A THOUSANDS OF CASTS
in SCATHING CYNICOLOR
SHE WAS THE

VAVA VOOM the POW girl?
WHEN HE SAW HER HE KNEW IT WAS WORTH SLOGGING THROUGH THE MUD!
HER LIPS SPOKE TENDER WORDS... "HEY JOE, YOU GOT GUM?"
HE WASN'T AFRAID OF BULLETS BUT HE WAS AFRAID OF HER!
ON OUR GREAT WIDE PANORAMIC STAGE - in person - THE FRAMIC FIVE!
Screenplay by - BENTLEY FLUD
From the play by - FLUDNEY BENT
From the novel by - BUDNEY FLENT
Original story by - FLENTNEY BUD
From the poem by - BEDNEY BUNT
From the speech by - FLEDNY FUNT
13¢ TILL NOON
$1.75 AFTER NOON
Plus - DOE JOKES specialty
Plus - Chapter Seven "Tarz an' the Apes"
Plus - Gifts
Plus - Souveniers
Plus - Money!
Plus
Hairy Hare

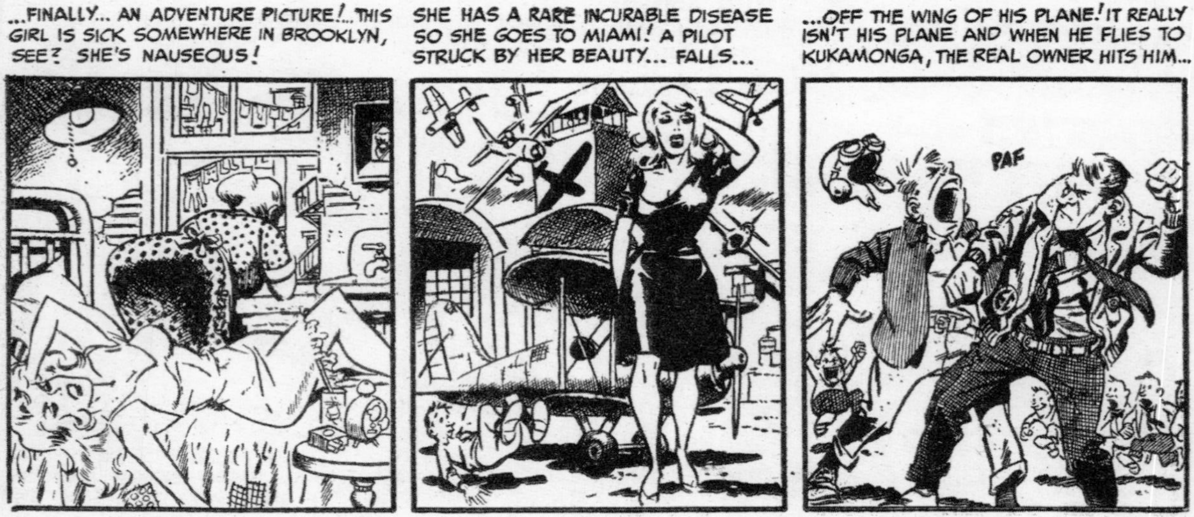
...FINALLY... AN ADVENTURE PICTURE!...THIS GIRL IS SICK SOMEWHERE IN BROOKLYN, SEE? SHE'S NAUSEOUS!
SHE HAS A RARE INCURABLE DISEASE SO SHE GOES TO MIAMI! A PILOT STRUCK BY HER BEAUTY... FALLS...
...OFF THE WING OF HIS PLANE! IT REALLY ISN'T HIS PLANE AND WHEN HE FLIES TO KUKAMONGA, THE REAL OWNER HITS HIM...
PAF

...BECAUSE HE'S SUCH A SLOPPY PILOT! ANYHOW...THE PILOT MEETS THE GIRL AGAIN IN BANFF, AT THE AQUARIUM...
SHE FLEES ON A BOAT TO POONA WHERE HE CATCHES HER AND AS SHE LEANS NAUSEOUS OVER THE RAIL...
...SHE TELLS HIM OF HER INCURABLE DISEASE! HE MARRIES HER ANYHOW! THEY GO TO SEE VESUVIUS ON THEIR HONEYMOON!
-Cola
GUIDED TOURS
SOUVENIERS

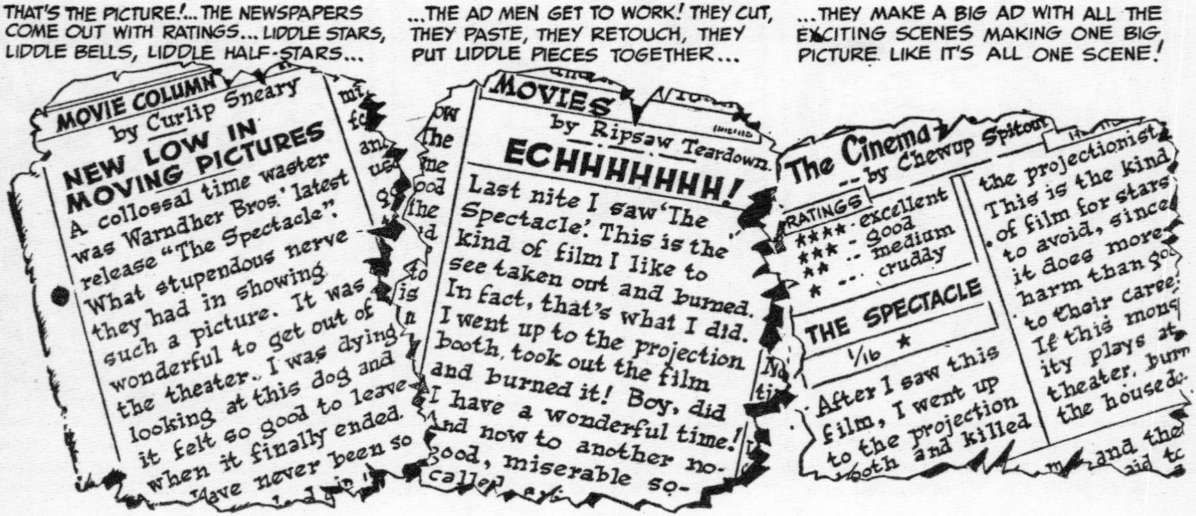
THAT'S THE PICTURE!... THE NEWSPAPERS COME OUT WITH RATINGS... LIDDLE STARS, LIDDLE BELLS, LIDDLE HALF-STARS...
...THE AD MEN GET TO WORK! THEY CUT, THEY PASTE, THEY RETOUCH, THEY PUT LIDDLE PIECES TOGETHER...
...THEY MAKE A BIG AD WITH ALL THE EXCITING SCENES MAKING ONE BIG PICTURE LIKE IT'S ALL ONE SCENE!
MOVIE COLUMN
by Curlip Sneary
NEW LOW IN MOVING PICTURES
A collossal time waster was Warndher Bros.' latest release "The Spectacle". What stupendous nerve they had in showing such a picture. It was wonderful to get out of the theater. I was dying looking at this dog and it felt so good to leave when it finally ended. have never been so
MOVIES
by Ripsaw Teardown.
ECHHHHHHHH!
Last nite I saw 'The Spectacle'. This is the kind of film I like to see taken out and burned. In fact, that's what I did. I went up to the projection booth, took out the film and burned it! Boy, did I have a wonderful time! and now to another no-good, miserable so-
The Cinema
-- by Chewup Spitout
RATINGS
**** - excellent
*** - good
** .. medium
* ... cruddy
THE SPECTACLE
1/16 *
After I saw this film, I went up to the projection booth and killed
the projectionist. This is the kind of film for stars to avoid, since it does more harm than good to their caree If this mong ity plays at theater, burn the house

...THOUSANDS OF MILES APART, THE
SCENES ARE TAKING PLACE...SO THEY
MAKE IT ONE SCENE... LIKE THIS...

SEE IT ON THE
CINAMORPHIC SCREEN
FILMED WITH
ANASCOPIC CAMERA
AND
STEREOPHONY SOUND
IN
GORIOUS SCHMEKNICOLOR
BY THE FRAZZLEDAZZIC LENS
SAZZAFRANIC SEATS
POPPAPHONIC POPCORN
WARNDHER BROS.
presents-
THE SPECTACLE
THE STORY OF A PAIR OF GLASSES
WORLD'S LARGEST DISTORTED SCREEN!

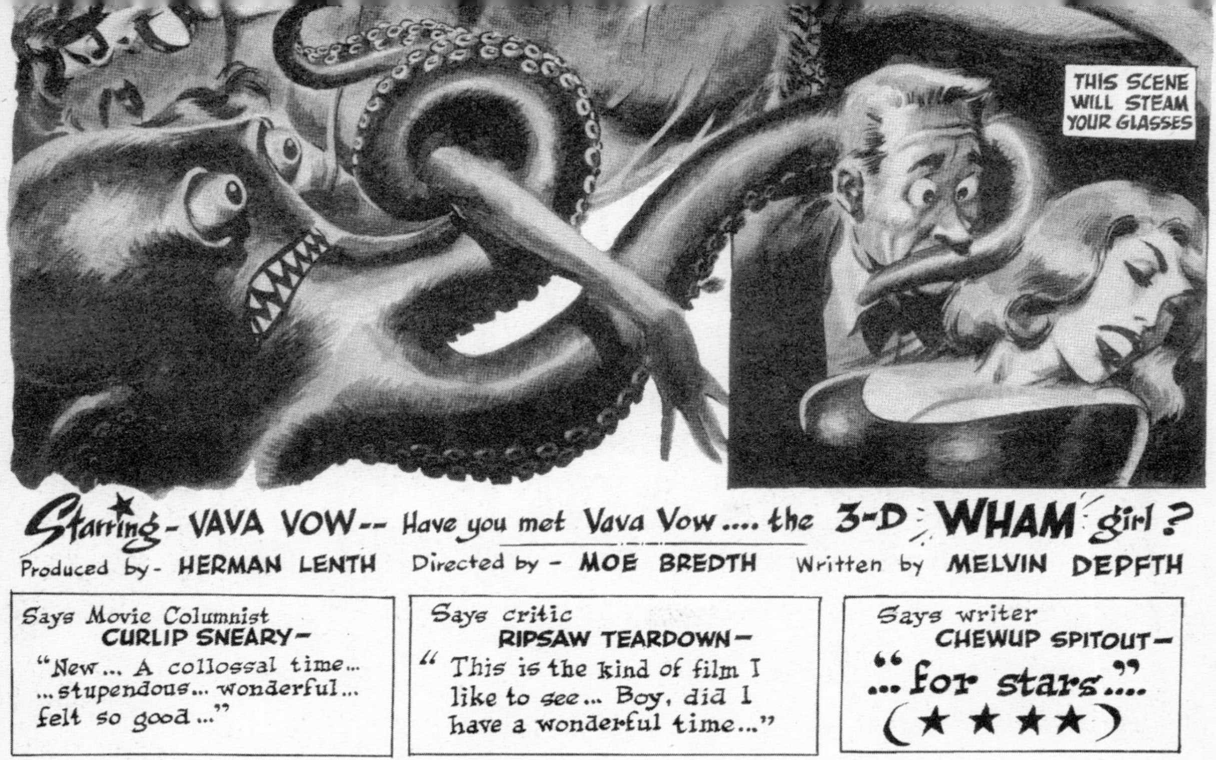
THIS SCENE WILL STEAM YOUR GLASSES
Starring - VAVA VOW -- Have you met Vava Vow .... the 3-D WHAM girl?
Produced by - HERMAN LENTH
Directed by - MOE BREDTH
Written by MELVIN DEPFTH
Says Movie Columnist CURLIP SNEARY -
"New ... A collossal time... ...stupendous... wonderful... felt so good..."
Says critic RIPSAW TEARDOWN -
"This is the kind of film I like to see... Boy, did I have a wonderful time..."
Says writer CHEWUP SPITOUT -
"...for stars...." (★★★★)

Newspaper Cartoon Dept.: Today we present two charming boys who for years have been making mischief on such a scale that although it isn't publicized, they have made their home a shambles and laid waste to the land! . . . Yes . . . You guessed it! . . .Those two lovable little rascals, Hans and Feetz . . .The . . .

KATCHANDHAMMER KIDS!

SCHOOL BU
SPEED LIMIT 250 M.P.H.
VILLY
ELDER

IN DER SEHN SUCHT NACH EINER HÖHER-EN EUROPÄISCHEN EINHEIT KLINGT HAUTE DER RUF DER DICHTER...
DER STAATS-MÄNNER UND IHRER VÖLKER ZUSAMEN!
DAS BESORGTE, UNGEDULDIGE DRÄNGEN DER JUGEND BEGLEITET DIE POLITISCHEN GESPRÄCHE...
UND VERHAND-LUNGEN, WEIL SIE BEFÜRCHTET, DASS DER...
SHULTZ HAS SVITCHT TO SHNOPPS!
...SHWUNG DER EURO-PÄISCHEN IDEE IM GESTRÜPP DER SCHWEI...
...RIGKEITEN ERLAHMEN KÖNNTE! ALLE DIESE DRÄNGENDEN HABEN RECHT. SIE GEBEN DEN...
REPENT! MAKE A PARSON TO PARSON CALL!!
EIN

DING
ACH DU LIEBER PFUI! DAS NEVER FAILEN! ALLES TIME ICH TAKEN MEIN SHOWER, DER TELEPHUNKEN GEHEN GERINGING!
BRUN HILDA
HEARTLINE: VENTRICAL-6-2211 FRAULINE: MARLENE 4-00000
GUTEN MORN-ING? IST DAS DER KAPITAN?
JA! DAS IST DER KAPITAN! WHO IST DAS?
... EXCUSE EIN MOMENTEN, KAPITAN, UBER COULD YOU HOLDEN DER WIRE EIN MOMENTEN?
JA ICH CAN HOLDEN ...UBER MACH SCHNELL!
STOP! DON'T LOOK! DON'T LISTEN! NUDEST CAMP AHEAD!
CURVES AHEAD..
BEWARE OF SOFT SHOULDERS!
NOTICE: ELDERLY WOMAN WITH HEARING AID WANTS TO MEET ELDERLY GENT WITH NEW BATTERY.

ACH DU LIEBER AUGUSTINE ... YUM TE TYUM TUM...
HOTEL CONRAD HINTON
DU...DU LICHTS MEIR IN HEARTZEN... TYUM TYUM TYUMTYUM TYA TUM...
HOTEL CONR HIN
DEUTCHLAND DEUTCHLAND UBER ALLES... TYATA TYUM TUM... TATYATA TUM...

HALLO, KAPITAN? IST DU STILL GEHOLDEN DER WIRE?
JA! ICH BEEN STILL GEHOLDEN DER WIRE! ICH BEEN GEHOLDEN DER DUM-BOOZLED WIRE FOR DER LASTEN ½ HOUR!
...DANKER-SCHOEN FUR HOLDEN DER WIRE!... GUTEN-BYE!
STOP!
DON'T
DON'T
CALL CUT-RATE FUNERAL PARLOR FOR OUR LAY-AWAY PLAN!
CADAVER 2-7643

...ICH HORT GE-FIGURED THEY HORT GEBEEN UP ZU MONKEY BUSINESS...
DANKERSHOEN INSPEKTOR! ICH VILLT GETEACHEN DEM FUR MACHEN MIR HOLDEN DER WIRE FUR ½ HOUR! ICH'LL WHALE DER TAR AUS FRUM DEM!
I CASH CLOTHES
SLEP! SMESH! ZETZ!
ZWEI

UBER KAPITAN, IST DAS DER BESTEN IDEA FUR TEACHING DER KINNDER TO BEHAVING?... TO WHALEN DER TAR AUS FRUM DEM?
YOU BETTEN! DAS IST DER ONLY WAY TO TEACHEN DEM NICHT TO MACHEN MONKEY BUSINESS!
UBER KAPITAN... THINKEN ZIE OF DER PSYCHO-LOGICAL RESULTEN!
ICH HORT GETHINKEN ONLY EINER THING... DER GAME OF GIN-RUMMY DU IST JOINING MEIR IN! COMEN ZIE INSIDE! ICH BETTER RINGEN DER DOORBELL FUR MAMMA TO OPENEN DER DOOR!
STAY OUT! GERMAN MEASLES
KAPITAN! WAS IST LOS?
ACH DU LIEBER! GETTEN MEIR LOOSE! DAS FURSHLUGGINER DOORBELL IST MACHEN MEIR AN ELECTRICITEN SHOCK!!
DZZZZZ

HOBOY, IST DAS KAPITAN GEGUNGEN ZU GEFEELEN SORRY!
VEN ICH IST GEFINISHED MIT EIM, DER KAPITAN IST **KAPUT!**
ALL DER VAY MIT ADLAI!
DEMERCRITIC PARTY
FSST

DU HORT GESHPRECHEN EIN MOUTHFUL, KIDDO!
GIDDYAPEN INTER DEN CLOSET, BOY! IST A SCHOEN APPLE IN DERE FUR DU!
DER CHAMPAGNE BOTTLE IST GEMACHEN READY!
TRY ENNDS MIT CHLOROPHYLL YET.

NURSERY
COMEN ZIE HEIR, FIDO!
HEIR IST EIN SCHOEN BONE FUR DU!
AIR RAID SHELTER
FSST!
NURSERY
RUMPUS
ROMPERS ROOM.
CHICKEE DER KAPITAN!
RAUSE OUTEN HEIR!
...ACH, JA, INSPEKTOR...DAS IST EIN SEHR IMPORTANT DAY FUR MEIR! DAS IST WHY ICH HORT GEPUTTEN ON MEIN BESTEN UNIFORMEN!
AIR RAID SHELTER
DREI

ICH HORT GEPUTTEN ON MEIN BESTEN UNIFORM FUR DAS REASON! AT LONGEN LAST, ICH HORT GEGOTTEN EIN OFFER ZU KOMMANDING EIN BOAT! ICH HORT GEWAITING YEARS FUR DAS OPPORTUNITY! DER BOAT KOMPANY IST GESENDING EIN MANN OVER TODAY FUR INTERVIEWEN ME UND ICH GOT ZU MACHEN EIN GUTEN IMPRESSION!
SKRITCH
SH! ...WAS IST DAS NOISE?
EAST ZONE
WEST ZONE
...DAS IST DER LASTEN OPPORTUNITY ICH VILT EVER HABEN ZU BE EIN REAL KAPITAN! ICH GOT ZU MACHEN EIN GUTEN IMPRESSION!
AHA! ICH HORT GE-THOUGHT ICH HORT GEHEARD A NOISE IN DEM CLOSET!
...DER KINNDER MACHEN MON-KEY BUSINESS! STEPPEN ZIE ASIDE UND ICH OPENEN DER DOOR!
DUN'T FORGET! NO PUTTING CHIKEN FET ON DER STER RALES MAMA.

RROWR
RRIP!
VOOF
POP!
KLOP
GO GO GO!

BALUMP
BALUMP
NOK
NOK

ER... EXCUSEN MEIR, MEIN HERR, UBER ICH AM GESEARCHING FUR DER KAPITAN!... ER... ICH HORT GEWONDERED IF DU KANST DIRECTEN MEIR ZU EIM!
ICH BIST DER KAPITAN!
...YOUCH?
...ICH!
...YOUCH?
...ICH!
...ECH!
HOO GE-SHTOLE DER DING DONG ?? MAMA.
FIER

KAPITAN! KAPITAN! DEIN BESTEN UNIFORM IST GETORN UND GESHTUNKEN MIT CHAMPAGNE! MACH SCHNELL UND CHANGE INTER DER NEXTEN BESTEN UNIFORM FUR DER IMPRESSION DU HAST GODT TO MACHEN ON DAS MANN DER BOAT KOMPANY IST GESENDING HEIR FUR INTERVIEWEN DU!
...BY DAS WAY... WHO VASST DAS?
...SNIFF!... DAS VASST DAS MANN DER BOAT KOMPANY IST GESENDING HEIR FUR INTERVIEWEN MEIR!
GESHTUNKENER DRUNK!

ICH HORT GEFOUNDEN DEM IM BALCONY IM DEIN ROXY THEATRE GELOOKEN AT DEM STAGE SHOW!
DANKERSHOEN, INSPEKTOR! ICH VILLT GIBEN ZU EIM EIN GROSSER SHOT IN DER KISHKERS... DASS VILLEN ZE NICHT FORGETTEN!
SMESH! SMESH!
PLASMA

...UBER KAPITAN, IST DU **SURE** DAS IST DER BESTEN IDEA FUR TEACHING DER KINNDER TO BEHAVING? DU HAST GEHEARD VAS SIGMUND FREUD HORT GESPOKEN...
HALTEN MIT DAS BENDEN OF MINE EAREN UND COMEN ZU PLAYING GIN-RUMMY! COMEN ZIE INSIDE!
CUPS
DAS SHOTTEN DER KINNDER IN DER KISHKERS IST GONNA GEMACHEN EIM SEHR WORSE! WASS DER KINNDER NEED IST DER LITTLE GELOVING UND LIKE DAS!
...UBER BEFORE ICH GERINGEN DOORBELL... ICH GEGOING TO PUTTEN ON DAS RUBBER GLOVES FUR INSULATION FRUM DAS ELECTRICITEN SHOCK!
KAPITAN! KAPITAN! WAS IST LOS?
GOTTEN HIMMEL! DAS FURSHLUGGINER DOORBELL AIN'T HABEN ELECTRICITEN SHOCK! DAS TIME IT HABEN POINTY NEEDLE STICKEN OUT!

FA HIMMEL SAKES... CURB YORE PARIKEETZ! DER KAPITAN
HOBOY, IST DAS KAPITAN GEGUNGEN ZU GETTEN IT!
...JA, BOY... RIGHT IM DER LABONZA, BOY!
GESOLINE
DAS IST DER TRICK, FIDO! STANDEN ZIE RIGHT HERE UND SHNAPPEN ZIE DAS TURTLE IF EIR HORT GESTICKEN DAS HEAD OUTEN DER SHELL!
MACHEN DAS PEA-SHOOTER AIMING AT FIDO WHILE ICH GE-FILLEN DAS FIREBUCKET MIT GASOLINEN!
FOR FIRE
OLINE
FOR SALE A KUPPLA NIZE, YUNG, HELTY AYRIAN BOYS!!
FUNF

ALLES IST GEFINISHED! CHEESE IT! ...DER KAPITAN!
...RAUSE OUTEN HEIR!
...ACH JA, MAMMA! ICH HORT JUST GECOMEN FRUM DER BANK, UND IN MIEN HANT IST DER LIFE SAVINGS FRUM DER LASTEN 30 YEARS!
THE NEW 'CHRISTIAN DIOR' SILHOUETTE FORM.
MIT DAS LIFE SAVINGS, DAS IST NOW POSSIBLE FUR US ZU MACHEN DER FONDEST DREAMS COMEN TRUE...ZU GEHEN OUDT FRUM DAS FARSHMMELT JUNGLE UND ZU GEHEN HOME ZU DER VATERLAND!
ACH... ICH BIST SEHR HAPPY!...UBER ICH GEHOPEN DAS LIFE SAVINGS IST SAFE IN DAS VASE DU IST GEPUTTEN DAS IN!
CHILDREN SHOOD BE SEEN UND NOT HURT! H.&F.
FIRST AID FOR PAPA.

HOME - (SOMETIMES NOT ZO SVEET.) HOME!
POOF
POOF
REST ROOMS
SPEED LIMIT 20 MILES P.H.
PINOCLE GAME IN DER BEER GARDEN TONITE

KING FARIKT BUYS BROOKLYN BRIDGE!
POT CHEESE
FOR FIRE
FOOMF!
ZEX

DAS FOOMF! VAS IST DAS FOOMF ICH HORT GEHEARD? IST DER FURNITURE GEBURNED? IST DER HOUSE ZUBROKEN? VAS IST DAS FOOMF?
DAS FOOMF ISS NICHT DER FURNITURE... DAS FOOMF ISS NICHT DAS HOUSE!... DAS FOOMF IST MERELY DAS L-LIFE (SNIFF) S-S-SAVINGS!
FOR FIRE
GRILLED CHEESE
ICH. HORT GEFOUNDEN DEM ON DER BACK DEN TROLLEY KAR GEHITCHING RIDES!
DANKERSHOEN, INSPEKTOR! ...DAS TIME ICH AM GAGOING ZU GIVEN EIM SUCH A BLITZ-KRIEG, DER KOPF IST GETTING ZUBROKEN!

...UBER KAPITAN, IST DU POSITIVEN DU IST DOING DER RICHTIKER THING? CANST DU NICHT SEEIN DAS DER MORE BEATING UND DER MORE HITTING DU HORT GEGIVEN DER KINNDER... DER MORE MONKEY BUSINESS EIR GEMAKES?
ACH, INSPEKTOR, ICH GUESS DU IST RICHT! DER BEATING MACHT DER KINNDER SEHR VICIOUS UND DAS ISS NICHT GUTE! UBER, WASS CAN ICH DO?
HALTEN DER HITTEN UND TAKEN HANZ UND FEETZ TO DER KINNDER PSYCHIATRIST FUR DER CONSULTATION!
...UBER LET'S FACE IT! MIT HITTEN HALTEN, DER MONKEY BUSINESS IS HALTEN!... MIT DER MONKEY BUSINESS HALTEN... DAS COMIC STRIP IST **KAPUT!**
NOTICE: GARBAGE MAN- PLIZ DUNT DELIVER ANYMORE GARBAGE DIS WEEK —MAMA
DAS IST NO LIE!
...WOOPS!...EIN MOMEN-TEN! BEFORE ICH PUSHEN DAS DOORBELL AGAIN, ICH GOTTA WATCHEN OUDT FUR DER ELECTRICITEN SHOCK ***UND*** DER POINTY NEEDLE... UND SO...
PLEASE- NO MORE DIAPER SERVICE FRUM NOW ON! MAMA

...ICH HABEN DER BESTEN IDEA!... ICH GONNA PUSHEN DOORBELL BUTTON, NICHT MIT DER HUMAN HANDEN... ICH GONNA PUSHEN DER BUTTON MIT DER STICK! MIT DAS WAY NIEN MONKEY BUSINESS CAN...
NOT RESPONSIBL FOR GUESTS REMAINING OVERNITE! MAMA. HANS FEETZ VILLY ELDER
SKIZZIK
...HAPPEN...
GE-BOOM!
ZIBBEN

MANY YEARS LATER...
ACH DU LIEBER, MOMMA... ICH ARE BECOMEN OLD! DAS IST GUTE ZU HABEN EIN DAY OF PEACE MITOUDT DER KINNDER IN DER HOUSE MACHEN MONKEY BUSINESS!... ICH HORT GEWONDERING WHERE IST DER INSPEKTOR FUR DER LASTEN COUPLE YEARS?
NOK NOK
...VAS IST LOS? ICH HORT GE-HEARD EIN KNOCKING IM DER DOOR!
EARTH, VENUS AND MARS SIGN PEACE PACT
GUTEN TAG, KAPITAN! HOW IST DU, DU OLD DUMKOPF!
INSPEKTOR, DU OLD SCHWEIN-HUNT!... ICH HORT JUST GETALKING ABOUT DU? ICH HORT NICHT GESEEN DU IN EIN DACHSHUND'S AGE!

UND HOW IST ALLER FAMILY? HOW IST HANZ UND FEETZ? UBER EIR HORT GEGROWN UP I'LL BETCHA!
JA!... DER KINNDER ISS OUDT UN DEM CAR... OOPS! ICH HORT GEHEARING THEM COMEN UN ZIE BACK DOOR!
VRRUMMM
SKWEEE!
EIR IST UPSTAIRS! COMEN UND SAY GUTEN TAG ZU EIM! ... REMEMBER HOW DU HAST GESPRECHEN ZU MEIR LONG AGO UBER HOW ICH SHOULD TAKEN DER KINNDER ZU DER PSYCHIATRIST?
PLEASE CLOSE MANHOLE COVER BEHIND YOU AFTER LEAVING. DENKS! MAMA.
... REMEMBER HOW DU HAST GESPRECHEN UND TELLEN MEIR DAS BEATING ISS NICHT GUTE... MACHEN DER KINNDER RESENTEN DER PARENTAL AUTHORITY ISS NICHT GUTE?
...HEIR IST DER BOYS ROOM!
ACH DU LIEBER! IST DAS DER BOYS? EIR IST GEGROWN INZER MENN!

JA! EIR HORT GEGROWN INZER MENN... UND AS FUR VAS DU HORT GESPRECHEN ZU ME LONG AGO, YOU KNOW...
...ICH ARE BEGINNEN ZU THINKEN DU WERE **RIGHT!**
OUR FOIST CRIME:
CERTIFICATE OF BIRTH HANS FEETZ
VIOLATION
OCHT

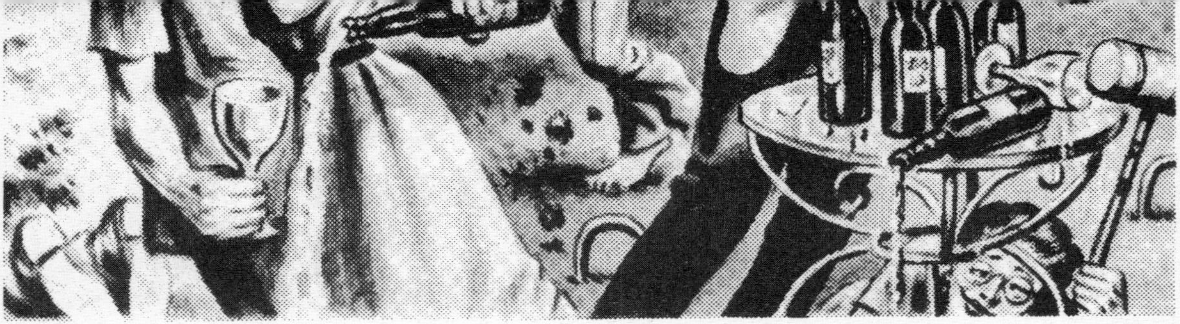

"PLAYING CROQUET ON THE FRONT LAWN," by Bill Elder. Number 1 in the series "Booze Life in America."

In this friendly, freedom-loving land
of ours–***beer belongs . . . enjoy it!***

Beer and ale—
mealtime favorites

AMERICA'S BEVERAGE OF MODERATION

Sponsored by the Brewer's Foundation to Encourage Excess

Hero Worship Dept.: You have heard of those two masked batlike crime fighters of Gotham City. . . . You have heard of their exciting deeds, of their constant war against the underworld! . . . This story, then . . . This story, then . . . has *absolutely nothing* to do with them! This story is about two different people. . . .

BAT BOY AND RUBIN!

PAF
NOTICE! THIS STORY IS A LAMPOON! IF YOU WANT TO SPEND YOUR DIME ON CHEAP, ROTTEN LAMPOONS LIKE THIS INSTEAD OF THE EVER-LOVIN' GENUINE, REAL THING... GO RIGHT AHEAD, BOY!
wood.

BAT BOY! BAT BOY! THE WHOLE GANG OF CROOKS IS GETTING READY TO **CHARGE!** SHOULD WE:
(a) FIGHT 'EM WITH OUR FISTS?
(b) FIGHT 'EM WITH OUR WEAPONS?
(c) RUN?
I'LL TELL YOU WHAT WE SHALL DO, RUBIN! WE SHALL DO THE **MORAL** THING, THE **NOBLE** THING, THE THING OUR PUBLIC WOULD **EXPECT** US TO DO!
...WE RUN!
...BUT **WAIT...**

...IT JUST SO HAPPENS I HAVE HERE IN ONE OF THE LITTLE COMPARTMENTS OF MY WEAPON'S BELT, A TINY VIAL OF SECRET GAS THAT PARALYZES GANGSTERS **JUST** LONG ENOUGH TO TAKE THEM AWAY TO JAIL!
TSSSS

WOW, BAT BOY! I THOUGHT YOU ONLY CARRIED A TINY VIAL OF SECRET GAS THAT BLINDS GANGSTERS AND A TINY VIAL OF SECRET GAS THAT TURNS GANGSTERS FRIENDLY... BUT NOT A TINY VIAL OF SECRET GAS THAT **PARALYZES** GANGSTERS!
HALP!
NOTE: WE REPEAT! LAMPOON! BATBOY MIT A BOY! RUBIN MIT A U!

KOF
KOF
AK!
KOF
KOF
KOF
(UGH)...(UGH)... I CAN'T SEEM TO FIND MY TINY LITTLE VIAL WHERE I KEEP MY FURSHLUGGINER SECRET GAS MASK... (UGH)...
...WELL... THAT FINISHES THE FLOOGLE GANG! LET'S CLIMB INTO THE SECRET BAT-O-MOBILE AND GO HOME!
MCXIII

WITH THE CLEANING UP OF THE FLOOGLE GANG, WE HAVE PROBABLY ENDED THE WAVE OF MYSTERIOUS KILLINGS THAT HAVE PLAGUED COSMOPOLIS CITY!
(COUGH) (COUGH) ...DRATTED SECRET GAS! ...HAND ME A KLEENEX FROM THE GLOVE COMPARTMENT, WILL YOU, RUBE?!
CHUG
PAF
POF!
GA GOO GA!
CHUG
QUEEK
CHUG
BAT BOY! BAT BOY! BAT BOY! ...L-LOOK WHAT'S IN THE GLOVE COMPARTMENT! A...A...A... THAT'S IT! A ROAD MAP FROM THE A.A.A.... AND A PAIR OF GLOVES!
SO WHAT? DIDN'T YOU EVER SEE GLOVES IN A GLOVE COMPARTMENT?
...WITH HANDS IN 'EM?

A BODY!... KILLED IN THE SAME MANNER AS ALL THE OTHERS! THE KILLER IS STILL AT LARGE!
QUICKLY!... ONTO OUR SECRET BAT-O-CYCLE! OBVIOUSLY THE KILLINGS WERE NOT THE WORK OF THE **FLOOGLE** GANG BUT I THINK THEY'RE THE WORK OF THE **FLEAGLE** GANG!
... NOW TO TAKE OUT MY SECRET BAT-O-LARIET...

... I THINK WE SHOULD DO SOME SWINGING FROM SKYSCRAPERS! ... DEFTLY, I SHAKE THE LARIET OUT OF ITS VIAL!... DEFTLY I AIM IT TOWARDS THAT POST, AND DEFTLY, I THROW IT WITH UNERRING AIM...
WOW!
OOP! MISSED!
... TAKE 'ER AROUND AGAIN!
BROOM
POK
BR-RUP
2

MISSED AGAIN!
ZOOM
MISSED!
ZIP
MISSED!
SWISH
MISSED!
VOOM!

... DEFTLY, I CLAMBER UP THE WALL TO THE POST AND I DEFTLY PLACE THE LOOP OVER THE POST AND PULL IT TIGHT WITH A DEFT JERK!
...O.K., YOU DEFT JERK! LET'S GO INTO OUR ROUTINE! ...WE GOTTA SWING UP TO THE SKY-SCRAPER TOP!
UP HA
HUP
HOO
HEY
HUP!
HO
HEP
WHEE
HIP
HE!
HEY!
LE'S GO!
HOO!
HUP!
O.K.! HERE GOES! UP TO THE SKYSCRAPER TOP! STAND BACK, EVERY-ONE!... WAY UP TO THE VERY TOP WE GO!
HOO BOY!
HEY
WEE-OOP!
ALLEZ
WHEE
HA
OOP!
YEY
HUP
HO
HA HOO
HE HE!
WEE!
HUP
HEP
HUP
HOO
HA
GERONIMO!
HA HOO
HO!

WOOD
KA-RUMF!
WHEE!
WELL, WE DIDN'T MAKE IT TO THE TOP, BUT WE GOT TO THE FIRST FLOOR!
WEE HA! HOO HEY HA HOO
...UH OH!... LOOK! BY SOME STRANGE COINCIDENCE, WE HAVE BLUNDERED INTO THE HEADQUARTERS OF THE MOST HORRIBLE... FEARSOME... FRIGHTENING... TOUGHEST GANG IN HISTORY!... THE FLEAGLE GANG!
CHIRP CHIRP
3

... THE F-FLEAGLE G-GANG! ...MOST TOUGHEST G-GANG OF D-DEAD-END KIDS IN CO-CO-CO-COSMOPOLIS!
WHAT DO YOU SAY, BAT BOY, SHOULD WE TAKE 'EM ON?
HOTE-EL-AY-EM-POON LAMPOON!
FLEAGLE CLUB SOCIAL AND RECRE
OF COURSE NOT, YOU STUPID FOOL! CAN'T YOU SEE WE'RE OUT-NUMBERED?
BUT BAT BOY, BO'!... THEY'RE PULLING THEIR ZIP-GUNS!... HAVEN'T YOU GOT SOME KIND OF LI'L OL' TINY VIAL OF SECRET GAS IN YOUR BELT TO STOP 'EM?

O.K..! HERE GOES TINY VIAL NUMBER 1!... A SECRET GAS THAT RIDS THE BODY OF OFFENDING ODORS AND... **OOP!** WAIT A MINUTE!.. THIS IS MY 'ARRID' SPRAY DEODORANT!
TSSS
THEY'RE STILL COMING! ...O.K..! HERE GOES TINY VIAL NUMBER 2! A SECRET GAS THAT MAKES CROOKS THINK THEY'RE COPS, AND THEY PUT THEMSELVES IN JAIL!
FOOSH
THEY'RE STILL COMING! ... O.K..! HERE GOES TINY VIAL NUMBER 3! ... IT FIRES A SECRET 9 INCH SELF-PROPELLED ARTILLERY SHELL!
BOOM
THEY'RE STILL COMING! ... BOY! IS THAT GANG TOUGH!... NOW I TRY THE SECRETEST VIAL OF ALL WITH A SECRET WEAPON THAT IS **BOUND** TO STOP THE FLEAGLE GANG...

...TINY FOLDED HAIR BRUSHES THAT, WHEN UNFOLDED, ARE FULL SIZE AND YOU CAN GIVE A GOOD WALLOP WITH! IF THESE KIDS WEREN'T DEAD-END KIDS BEFORE... THEY'LL BE DEAD-END KIDS NOW!... BOY! WILL THEIR ENDS BE DEAD!
to lampoon is human, to forgive divine
OW YOW!
WHAA
THE FLEAGLE GANG IS FINISHED! THERE WILL BE NO MORE MURDERS IN COSMOPOLIS! NOW! ONTO THE WINDOW SILL! FASTER THAN A SPEEDING BULLET, KAPWEENG! UP... UP... UP... UP AND AWAY!
WAIT A MINUTE, BAT BOY! THAT 'FASTER THAN A SPEEDING BULLET' IS ANOTHER CHARACTER'S ROUTINE!... IT MAY BE COPYRIGHTED! WANT TO GET US SUED?
4

...AND NOW... WE DEFTLY SWING OUT ON OUR ROPE... **HEY! SOMEONE ELSE IS SWINGING ON THIS ROPE!**
HA BOY! WHAT A CLUMSY DOPE... TRYING TO HORN IN ON OUR ACT! WHO EVER HEARD OF SWINGING ON A ROPE BY THE NECK!
note: ANY SIMILARITY BETWEEN THIS LAMPOON AND ANY OTHER LAMPOON IS STRICTLY A LAMPOON.
?
?
BY THE NEECK? ...THIS IS OBVIOUSLY THE WORK OF THE SAME MURDERER OF THE OTHER BODIES!...QUICK!...ONTO THE BAT-O-WAGON!
WANTED
THE BLUE BUG
...THERE IS ONLY ONE GANG LEFT IN COSMOPOLIS THAT COULD'VE DONE THIS... THE **FLURGLE** GANG!... NOW I DEFTLY TOSS A ROPE...

...HERE WE GO DOWN TO THE HIDEOUT OF THE FLURGLE GANG...
HUP
WHEE!
ALLEZ OOP!
HEY-UP!
LE'S GO!
HOOPLA!
HOO HEY HA
OOPS!
SCREECH!
HIP!
HO!
HUP
HEP!
LE'S GO!
HUP!
HEY UP!

NOW WHAT? WE CAN'T SWING IN EITHER DIRECTION BECAUSE WE'VE LOST MOMENTUM! I HAD THIS WHOLE BOTTLE FULL OF MOMENTUM IN MY POCKET AND I LOST IT!... WHAT DO WE DO NOW?
... THE ANSWER IS SIMPLE, RUBIN! ONE HAS MERELY TO LET GO OF THE ROPE AND DROP DEFTLY TO THE GROUND...
CRASH
CRUNCH!
BDOINKS
BA-DOINK!
TOINGG
...OF COURSE ... THE SHOCK OF THE 20 STORY FALL TO THE GROUND IS TAKEN UP BY THE SECRET SPRINGS ONE HAS IN THE TINY VIALS OF THE WEAPONS BELT... THAT IS... IF ONE **HAS** A WEAPONS BELT!
5

COME ON, RUBIN! THERE'S THE FLURGLE GANG! CHARGE!
LOOK, GANG-MEMBERS! HERE COMES BAT BOY AND RUBIN! SHOOT 'EM DOWN!
BA DA BAM
BOOM
PAF BLAM
MISSED!
POW BAM
POP
MISSED!
BRRT
KA POW
MISSED!
MISSED! MISSED! MISSED!
MISSED!
POOR FOOLS! DON'T YOU KNOW US COMIC BOOK CHARACTERS ARE ALWAYS MISSED WHEN WE RUN AT THE GUNS?
BAM
BOM
POW
BANG
PRRT
POF

LOOK! THE FLURGLE GANG IS MADE UP OF WOMEN!... QUICK LEMME AT MY GAS VIALS!
GAS VIALS! YOU WOULDN'T USE GAS VIALS ON WOMEN WOULD YOU, BAT BOY?
HANDS OFF, YOU DUMKOPF... I'M LOOKING FOR MY SECRET VIAL OF 'ARRID' SPRAY DEODORANT!
PUT AWAY YOUR VIALS, YOUR WEAPONS, YOUR MECHANICAL DEVICES! THIS SITUATION CALLS FOR HAND-TO-HAND COMBAT!... MAINLY WRASSLING!
RIGHT!

CRUNCH
EEK
HOO HA!
SNAP CRACKLE POP!
THUD
OW
R-RIP!
thud!
OW
LEGGO!
KA-PWEENG!
ZOW
THUD!
BASH
EEK
SCHMEK!
OY!

TAKE OUT YOUR VIALS, YOUR WEAPONS, YOUR MECHANICAL DEVICES! THIS SITUATION CALLS FOR FOUL BLOWS, DIRTY FIGHTING, ATROCITIES! THIS MEANS **WOAH!**
NOTE: NOT A SPITTOON NOT A CARTOON NOT A HARPOON BUT A LAMPOON!
...LET 'EM HAVE IT, BAT BOY!
6

WELL-P... THAT TAKES CARE OF THE FLURGLE GANG!... THERE ARE NO MORE GANGS LEFT IN COSMOPOLIS! THERE WILL BE NO MORE MURDERS! LETS HOP ONTO OUR BAT-O-CYCLES AND PEDAL HOME TO HEADQUARTERS!
PHEW! WHAT A DAY! SOMETIMES I WONDER, SINCE YOU ARE A WEALTHY YOUNG SOCIALITE IN REAL LIFE, WHY YOU KEEP KNOCKING YOURSELF OUT ON THIS 'BAT BOY' KICK! IT DON'T PAY, YOU KNOW!
RUBIN! THERE ARE OTHER THINGS IN LIFE BESIDES MONEY... FINER THINGS! ...THINGS THAT CANNOT BE BOUGHT... THINGS MUCH BETTER! FINER THAN MONEY!... THINGS LIKE... LIKE... LIKE POWER! RRROW! WURF! GRRR!
...NOW HANG UP MY CAPE LIKE A GOOD FELLOW!
HQ

HANG UP MY CAPE WHILE I TAKE A NAP, KID! CALL ME IF ANY CRIMINALS START FOOLING AROUND IN COSMOPOLIS!
TAKING YOUR NAP IN YOUR USUAL BAT POSITION, EH, BATBOY? ...I'LL JUST HANG YOUR CAPE IN YOUR CLOSET AND...
EEK!
THUD
ANOTHER DEAD BODY... KILLED IN THE SAME WAY AS THE OTHERS! THE FLOOGLE GANG IS WIPED OUT! THE FLEAGLE GANG IS WIPED OUT! THE FLURGLE GANG IS WIPED OUT!... THEN THE MURDERER CAN ONLY BE ONE OTHER PERSON... ONE OTHER PERSON... ONE CRAZY MIXED UP KID... AND THAT IS... IS... IS...
SMASH!

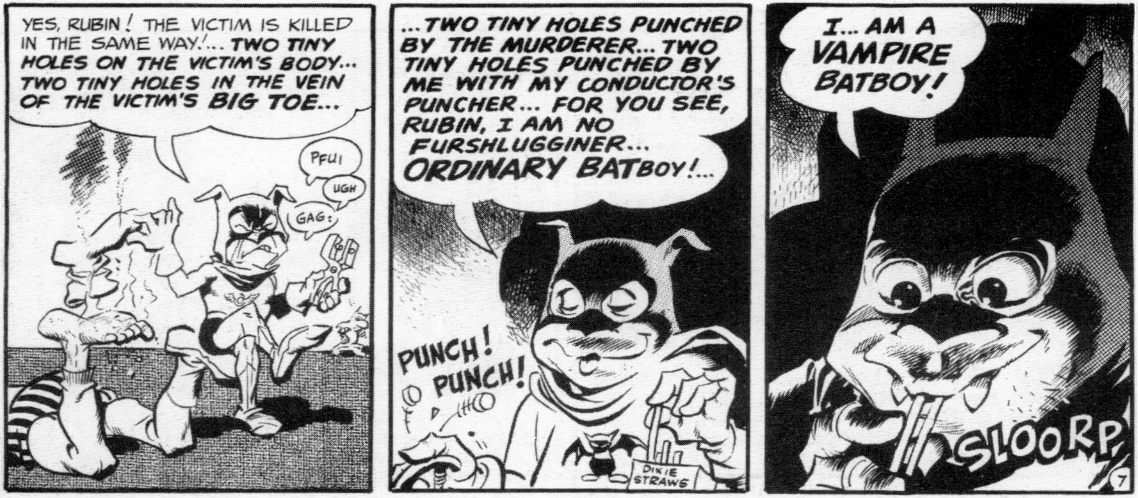
YES, RUBIN! THE VICTIM IS KILLED IN THE SAME WAY!... TWO TINY HOLES ON THE VICTIM'S BODY... TWO TINY HOLES IN THE VEIN OF THE VICTIM'S BIG TOE...
PFUI
UGH
GAG:
...TWO TINY HOLES PUNCHED BY THE MURDERER... TWO TINY HOLES PUNCHED BY ME WITH MY CONDUCTOR'S PUNCHER... FOR YOU SEE, RUBIN, I AM NO FURSHLUGGINER... ORDINARY BATBOY!...
PUNCH!
PUNCH!
DIXIE STRAWS
I... AM A VAMPIRE BATBOY!
SLOORP
7

WHAT'S WRONG WITH THIS PICTURE?

HAVING FUN, GANG?... BET YOU ARE... MAINLY SINCE THIS IS THE LAST NAUSEATING PAGE IN THIS PUZZLE-PAGE FIASCO! IN THE FOLLOWING PICTURES, THE ARTIST HAS MADE A NUMBER OF MISTAKES! SEE IF YOU CAN FIND AND LIST THEM!...NEEDLESS TO SAY, THE ARTIST WILL BE FIRED AS PROMPTLY AS POSSIBLE SINCE THIS COMPANY DOES VERY GOOD, HIGH-CLASS ART WORK USING ONLY THE BEST AND WE KICK OUT ALL ARTISTS WHO MAKE MISTAKES!

WHAT'S WRONG WITH THIS PICTURE?

1.

ANSWERS ON LAST PAGE!

A fog lies thick on London, giving a lonely, eerie quality to the night sounds! . . . The ominous chiming of Big Ben . . . the footsteps of some*thing* scuttling by . . . the hollow clack of Dr. Whatsit's head coming in contact with a lamppost as he rushes through the fog to see his old friend . . .

SHERMLOCK SHOMES!

RAP!
?
BILL ELDER

DRAT! WHERE IS SHOMES?
AHOY THERE! WE'VE BEEN SAILING FOR DAYS! COULD YOU DIRECT US TO PING-PONG ISLAND?
EASY ST.
EASIEST ST.
GAD!... EVEN THE BOATS ARE LOST IN THIS DRATTED PEA-SOUP FOG!
WHERE THE DEVIL IS SHOMES?
FLUP!
EASILY ST.
UNEASY ST.
SPEAKEASY ST.
SKID ROW
SLIPPERY ROW
SLIMY ROW
OHO! I SAY, BY JOVE, HYAR IT IS SHO' NUFF! 2½ BAKER STREET... I WONDER IF HERMLOCK IS SHOME ... ER ... ER ... IF SHERMLOCK IS HOME...?
SLICK ROW
SLIDE RULE ROW
MARILYN MON ROW
SYDNEY GREEN STREET
COOK ST.
CHEF ST.
BAKER ST.
21/2
1

AHA! THERE'S THE OLD RASCAL'S SHADOW ON THE WINDOW SHADE NOW, SMOKING HIS SHAG TOBACCO ... A PERFECT TARGET FOR ARTY-MORTY, SHOMES'S ARCH-ENEMY!
BY JOVE! THERE'S ARTY-MORTY NOW!
WE HAVE BOUGHT GIRL SCOUT COOKIES
BLAM
BLIM
BLAM
...LITTLE DOES ARTY-MORTY KNOW THAT THAT SHADOW IS MERELY CAST ON THE WINDOW SHADE BY A LIFELESS STATUE... A REPLICA OF SHERMLOCK SHOMES!

AH, SHOMES! PLAYING THE VIOLIN AS USUAL TO HELP YOU THINK!
CLEVER TRICK THAT... CASTING A SHADE SHADOW OF SHERMLOCK SHOMES WITH A SHTATSHUE SHTANDING ON A SHABLE... BLFT... SPUT... I MEAN **TABLE!**

...LITTLE DID ARTY-MORTY KNOW THAT THAT SHADOW IS MERELY CAST BY A LIFELESS STATUE... A REPLICA OF YOURSELF!
...WRONG AGAIN, WHATSIT!

THE STATUE IS REAL!.. THE VIOLIN PLAYER IS A LIFELESS STATUE... A REPLICA OF MYSELF, CLEVER-LY MANIPULATED BY WATCH-WORKS TO MOVE ABOUT AND TO PLAY THE VIOLIN!... ARTY-MORTY HAS FOILED ME AGAIN!
CLIK
RIP!

AHA, SHOMES! YOU'RE PUTTING VIOLIN TO CHIN! YOU'RE GOING TO THINK!...BY **JOVE! MY FAVORITE CLASSICAL TUNE..."DOGGIE IN THE WINDOW"!**
WHATSIT? WHAT IF I WAS TO TELL YOU THAT IN A FEW MINUTES WE SHALL HAVE A VISITOR...
2

...HOW MUCH IS THAT DOGGIE TYA TA DE TUM...
WHATSIT? WHAT IF I WAS TO TELL YOU OUR VISITOR WILL BE A FEMALE... WITH BLUE EYES... BLONDE HAIR IN A TWEED SUIT... TIGHT SKIRT... BLACK HIGH-HEELED PUMPS...
WURF! WURF!
CONFOUND IT, SHOMES! HOW THE DEUCE CAN YOU DEDEUCE ALL DIS?
SILK STOCKINGS... LONG EYELASHES... BRIGHT RED LIPS... A TERRIFIC BUIIT...
WHAT IF I WAS TO TELL YOU THAT SHE WILL KNOCK ON THE DOOR IN A MOMENT!
KNOK NOK!
COME IN, MY DEAR!
SLURP!

HO, HO! THAT'S RICH! IT'S MRS. GOWANUS, THE LAND-LADY!
OH DEARIE ME, MR. SHOMES! H'I DIDN' THINK YEW CARED... KISSIN' MY HAND LIKE THAT... AN' JUST AFTER ME CLEANIN' H'OUT THE CESS-POOL!
SACKS 10TH AVE.
WE'D MAKE A LUVLY COUPLE WE WOULD, MR SHOMES... YEW PLAYIN' THAT THERE BANJO WHILE I CLEAN H'OUT THE CESS-POOL!
EXCUSE ME, SIR! DOES SHERMLOCK SHOMES, PRIVATE EYE LIVE HERE?

HAH.! SEE? SEE?... JUST LIKE I TOLD YOU.!?... SEE?... FEMALE.!? BLONDE HAIR.!? SEE, BOY?... HAH.! DIDN' I TOLD YOU?... DIDN' I ??
RIP!
... MR. SHOMES...
...WAIT, MADAM... DON'T TELL ME WHY YOU CAME! LET ME MAKE A BRILLIANT DEDUCTION!... YOUR NAME IS LASSIE ROVER! YOU CAME TO TELL ME ABOUT YOUR UNCLE, ROLLOVER ROVER!... HIS LIFE IS IN DANGER!... THIS MORNING WHILE YOU WAITED FOR A 8:07 TRAIN IN CHARING CROSS STATION...
WURF! WURF!
RIP!
...BUT MR. SHOMES!
...BUT
...BUT
...BUT BUT...
3

...YOU WERE CHEWING ON A CHICLET AT THE TIME... TUTTI FRUTTI, I BELIEVE...
RIP!
WURF! WURF!
...BUT MR. SHOMES! I DIDN'T COME TO TELL YOU NUTTIN'! I'M JUST SELLING COOKIES...
...GIRL SCOUT COOKIES FROM DOOR TO DOOR! BUT I THINK YOU NEED YOUR MONEY MORE THAN THE GIRL SCOUTS!
...'BYE!
WURF! WURF!

GIRL SCOUT COOKIES! I CAN'T UNDERSTAND WHERE MY DEDUCTION WENT WRONG!
WURF! WURF!
...AND YET... SOMETHING BOTHERS ME AND I DON'T KNOW WHAT! ...AHA!... NOW I KNOW!... I'VE GOT MY LEFT SHOE ON MY RIGHT FOOT!
POW
...HUMM... WHAT WAS IT SHE SAID? HUMM!... WAIT A MINUTE! WHAT HAPPENS IF I TAKE THE FIRST LETTER FROM EACH WORD OF HER SENTENCE! BY JOVE... THAT SPELLS GSCFDTDBITYNYMMTTGS!
KIYI! KIYIYI!

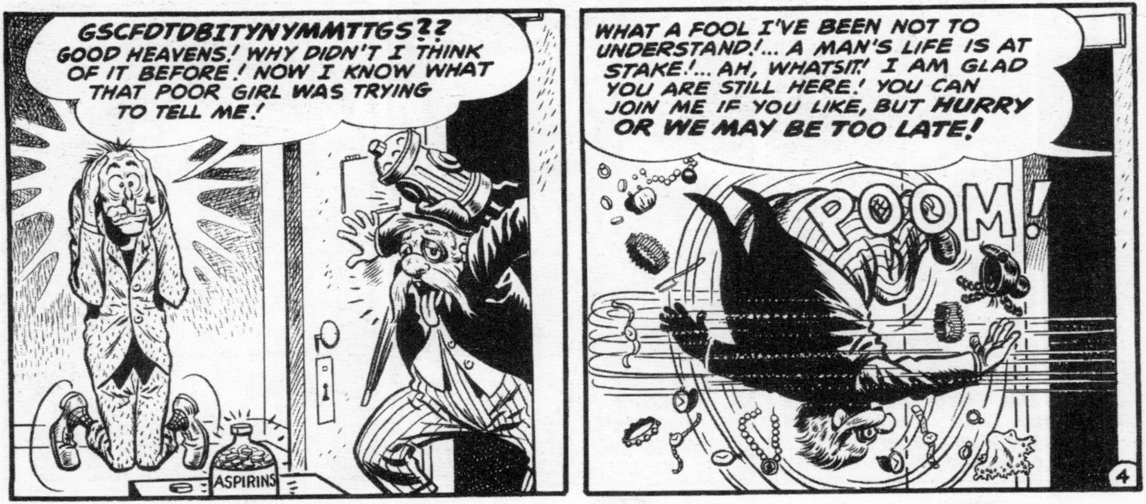
GSCFDTDBITYNYMMTTGS??
GOOD HEAVENS! WHY DIDN'T I THINK OF IT BEFORE! NOW I KNOW WHAT THAT POOR GIRL WAS TRYING TO TELL ME!
ASPIRINS
WHAT A FOOL I'VE BEEN NOT TO UNDERSTAND!... A MAN'S LIFE IS AT STAKE!... AH, WHATSIT! I AM GLAD YOU ARE STILL HERE! YOU CAN JOIN ME IF YOU LIKE, BUT HURRY OR WE MAY BE TOO LATE!
POOM!
4

I'LL NEVER FORGIVE MY-SELF IF WE'RE NOT IN TIME, WHATSIT! HURRY! HURRY, MAN!
5
5
SOAP BOX DERBY
P&G
PRAY, WHATSIT! PRAY THAT WE GET THERE IN TIME! PRAY THAT WE ARE NOT TOO LATE, FOR HEAVEN'S SAKE!
FULLY PACKED & EXTREMELY MILD
HUZZAH, WHATSIT! THERE'S THE PLACE UP AHEAD!... YOU THERE! TELL ME... T-TELL ME, ARE WE TOO LATE?
YES! YOU'RE TOO LATE!

3-DIMENSION "COWBOYS AND INDIANS."
THE MAIN FEATURE STARTED HALF AN HOUR AGO!
GET YOUR POLARIZED WIND SHIELDS FOR YOUR CAR - GOOD FOR 3-D DRIVE-IN THEATRES!
DASH IT ALL! AND IT WAS A THREE-D MOVIE TOO!
HIGH-HO! ...MIGHT AS WELL FOLLOW UP THE BLONDE IN THE TIGHT SKIRT!

AHA! MY SENSE OF DEDUCTION TELLS ME SHE LIVES HERE! RING THE BELL LIKE A GOOD FELLOW, WHATSIT!
...HA, MISS! WE MEET AGAIN!... YOU SHOULDN'T HAVE GONE SO QUICKLY! YOU SEE, I WAS THINKING OF PURCHASING A GIRL SCOUT COOKIE!
SLURP!

HO! MRS. GOWANUS AGAIN!
AWWWR! MR. SHOMES AGAIN! IT JUST SO 'APPENS I CLEAN H'OUT THE CESS-POOL 'ERE TOO!
MR. SHOMES! DR. WHATSIT! THANK HEAVENS YOU'RE HERE. COME IN!
MY UNCLE HAS BEEN IN HIS STUDY ALL DAY LONG! THE DOOR IS LOCKED! I CAN'T GET IN! I'VE TRIED EVERYTHING!
WURF WUP!
HUMM! ... WHAT ABOUT USING A KEY?
A KEY! GAD, MR SHOMES! I NEVER THOUGHT OF THAT!
5

WAIT! I JUST REMEMBER! THIS DOOR LOCKS FROM THE INSIDE ONLY!
VEDDY WELL! I SHALL HAVE TO RESORT TO MY PHYSICAL POWERS! BE A GOOD FELLOW AND GIVE ME A HAND, WHATSIT! HERE WE GO! ONE...TWO...
TALPS!
SPELLS 'SPLAT!' BACKWARDS.
...THRREE!
HA! ...GOOD SHOW, WHATSIT!

APPARENTLY IT WOULD DO BETTER FOR ME TO THROW **MY** WEIGHT FROM THE REAR!
HERE WE GO! ...ONE ...TWO ...THREE...
I ALWAYS SAID YOU WERE TOO FLABBY FOR YOUR OWN GOOD, WHATSIT! **THIS DOOR NEEDS A GOOD FIRM SHOULDER!** STEP OUT OF THE WAY PLEASE!
HERE WE GO AGAIN!
A-**ONE**... A-**TWO**... A-**THREE**...
ZZZZ

THIS CORD RINGS FOR THE MAID
THIS CORD RINGS FOR THE BUTLER!
OH NO!
HEAVEN PROTECT US!
SHET MAH MOUTH!
THIS IS THE LOST CORD!
THIS CORD IS A PAJAMAS BELT

... IT'S MY UNCLE!
...MURDERED!
IN A WINDOWLESS ROOM... LOCKED FROM THE INSIDE!
PEACE OF MIND
6

UH-OH! EVERYBODY LOOK OUT, 'CAUSE SHOMES IS SMOKING HIS FAVORITE SHAG TOBACCO AND FIDDLING HIS FAVORITE TUNE!
...VERY INTERESTING CASE, WHATSIT! IT WOULD SEEM THAT THE MURDERED MAN, AFTER LOCKING HIMSELF IN HIS STUDY, TRIPPED AND FELL AGAINST THE MANTLEPIECE... SMASHING HIS HEAD IN! IN OTHER WORDS... IT WAS MADE TO LOOK LIKE AN **ACCIDENT!**
WURF! WURF!

...BUT THERE IS SOMETHING VERY SUSPICIOUS ABOUT THIS ROOM!
...LET ME SEE NOW!
HMMM!
HUM!
AHA!
AHUM!
AH!
AHA!
UMHUM!
HOOHAH!
VOTE FOR STEVENSON
STEVENSON

IT IS EXACTLY AS I SUSPECTED!
JUST AS I SUSPECTED EXACTLY!
...AS I EXACTLY SUSPECTED... THERE ARE TERMITES IN THIS HOUSE!
...NOT THAT IT HAS ANYTHING TO DO WITH THIS CASE, BUT YOU SHOULD CATCH TERMITES BEFORE THEY BEGIN TO SWARM!

TO GET BACK TO THIS BORING OL' CASE, I WILL SHOW HOW THE VICTIM DID NOT, AFTER LOCKING HIMSELF IN HIS STUDY, TRIP AND FALL AGAINST THE MANTLEPIECE AND SMASH HIS HEAD IN AS IF IT WAS AN ACCIDENT!
WHATSIT! ...SIT IN THAT CHAIR, PLEASE!
TH- THE MURDERED MAN'S CHAIR?

HO HO!... COME NOW, WHATSIT! I'M JUST USING YOU TO ILLUSTRATE HOW THE MURDER HAPPENED! NOTHING CAN **POSSIBLY** HAPPEN TO YOU!
NOW!... YOUR UNCLE WAS NO DOUBT SITTING THERE IN HIS WING CHAIR!
THE MURDERER KNOWING YOUR UNCLE USUALLY RETIRED TO THE STUDY TO READ, ENTERED UNSEEN BY WAY OF... HEH... HEH... THE **CHIMNEY!**
THE ROARING FIRE IN THE FIRE-PLACE PRESENTED NO OBSTACLE SINCE THE MURDERER QUIETLY PUSHED THE LOGS ASIDE BEFORE COMING THROUGH!
7

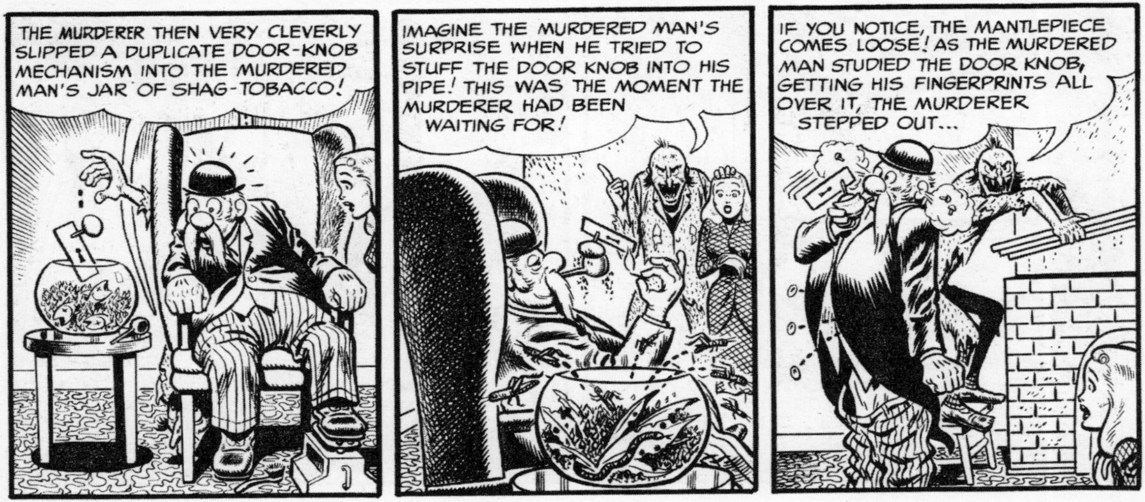
THE MURDERER THEN VERY CLEVERLY SLIPPED A DUPLICATE DOOR-KNOB MECHANISM INTO THE MURDERED MAN'S JAR OF SHAG-TOBACCO!
IMAGINE THE MURDERED MAN'S SURPRISE WHEN HE TRIED TO STUFF THE DOOR KNOB INTO HIS PIPE! THIS WAS THE MOMENT THE MURDERER HAD BEEN WAITING FOR!
IF YOU NOTICE, THE MANTLEPIECE COMES LOOSE! AS THE MURDERED MAN STUDIED THE DOOR KNOB, GETTING HIS FINGERPRINTS ALL OVER IT, THE MURDERER STEPPED OUT...

...AND DEFTLY BASHED THE VICTIM ON THE HEAD WITH THE MANTLEPIECE!
...THEN WITH GLOVED HANDS, HE SUBSTITUTED HIS DOOR-KNOB MECHANISM FOR THE REAL ONE!
!GNOB

THE MURDERER THEN LOCKED THE DOOR, REPLACED THE BURNING LOGS, AND STOLE QUIETLY UP THE CHIMNEY AND INTO THE NIGHT, MAKING IT LOOK AS IF THE MURDERED MAN, AFTER LOCKING HIMSELF IN HIS STUDY, TRIPPED AND FELL AGAINST THE MANTLEPIECE ... SMASHING HIS HEAD IN!

...AND THAT MURDERER IS YOU, MADAM... ARTY-MORTY IN DISGUISE!... CAH-MON, ARTY... TAKE OFF THAT WIG! SCOTLAND YARD IS ON THE WAY! YOU MIGHT AS WELL CONFESS!
STOP
HEY! ...HE'S CRAZY!
THE WAY I WAS KILLED... AFTER LOCKING MYSELF IN MY STUDY, I TRIPPED AND FELL AGAINST THE MANTLEPIECE... SMASHING MY HEAD IN! IT WAS AN ACCIDENT!
SHOMES! SCOTLAND YARD ARRESTS YOU FOR THE MURDER OF DR. WHATSIT! WE WARN YOU... ANYTHING YOU SAY WILL BE HELD AGAINST YOU!
GO
POLICY
AAA
MARILYN MONROE! ...LANA TURNER! ... HEDY LAMARR!
8

ANSWER PAGE
BILL ELDER DREWD THEM

DOT PICTURES

1.

2.

THE MAZE

PRETTY TOUGH PUZZLE, EH GANG? BUT THAT'S BECAUSE YOU DIDN'T FOLLOW THE DIRECTIONS... BECAUSE YOU WEREN'T SHARP-WITTED... BECAUSE YOU DIDN'T GO 'ROUND THE OUTSIDE AND COME IN OVER HERE...

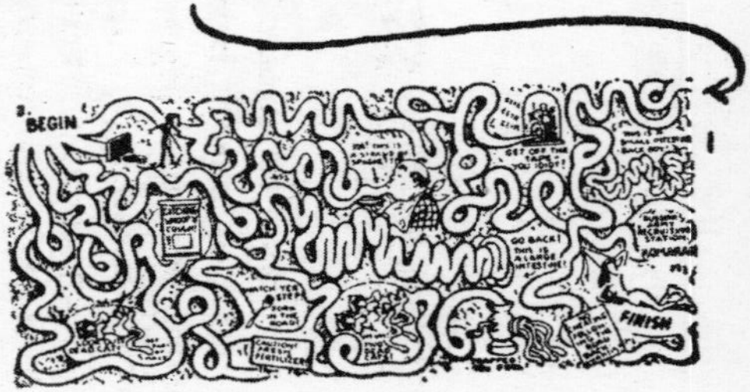

WHAT'S WRONG WITH THIS PICTURE?

BETTER STILL YOU SHOULD ASK... WHAT'S *RIGHT* WITH THIS PICTURE!!

BACKWORD BY STAN FREBERG

That fortunate legion of us tuned in on the MAD wave length, and therefore receptive to the mighty impulses radiating from its Furshlugginer-active[1] pages, will immediately recognize the wisdom of a Backword. I feel, therefore, that no explanation is necessary. True, a few preoccupied shoppers may whisk the book home thinking it is Norman Vincent Peale or at least "The Mollie Goldberg Cookbook." No matter. These people, being too pseudo-blasé or just plain dull to receive the MAD radiations, will (a) suffer an intense migraine headache four pages in, and (b) fling the book out the window.

So that takes care of *them.*

This leaves a number of non-MAD-addicts who, because of their superior intelligence, will (a) see instantly the brilliant lampoonery that is MAD, (b) curse themselves soundly for having been behind the door when MAD was handed out, and (c) howl all the way through. By the time they will have reached the Backword, their brain-pans will have been conditioned to accept such things without a question. They will have become "MADDICTS" and therefore one of us. And *we* don't need any explanation of a Backword, do we? So the sooner you get it through your potrzebie that there won't be any explanation the better—and that's final now! Crimenentles!

Where was I? Oh, yes, the Backword. For the uninformed, MAD started out three years ago as a comic book kidding only other comic strips. It has graduated today into a first-rate humor magazine, kidding not only comic strips but movies, TV, novels, commercial ads or anything it feels like. Merely to say that I am a fan of this magazine would be like saying that Gina Lollo-

[1]Similar to "radio-active" but with fewer commercials.

brigida is "sort of interesting." I am addicted to MAD like the Aga Khan to starches. Why? Because it makes me laugh, and I am rather fond of laughing.

Fortunately, MAD loves to laugh at the same things I do—that is to say, we are both completely insane. MAD does the same thing in a literary (or illiterary) form that I try to do on phonograph records, which is to point up some of the absurdities of mankind through the medium of satire. In a world where things get a shade ridiculous at times, satire is a very important thing to mental health. It lets a little of the air out of people and things who take themselves too seriously and deserve to be brought back down to earth. It also gives everyone a good healthy laugh into the bargain.

MAD is an example of pure and honest satire, written brilliantly by my friend Harvey Kurtzman, and drawn hysterically by Jack Davis, Bill Elder and Wallace Wood. I cannot praise their combined efforts enough. This volume, for example, is taken from several issues of the original MAD and is all written by Harvey. My favorite is "Smilin' Melvin." You may like "Superduperman."[2]

In closing, let us remember that someone once said "Laughter is the best medicine." It is a true fact that a friend of mine had an acquaintance who fell into poor health and proceeded to decline a little each day until the doctors could do nothing for him. Upon being told that the patient was beyond medical help, my friend called one day at his bedside and on a hunch told him a very funny joke he had just heard regarding three wild animals and a man who played the violin.[3] As he reached the punch line, the pale man opened his eyes and laughed for the first time in months. Color returned to his face, and would you believe it?—within forty-eight hours . . . he was dead. The laughter had overtaxed him. This shows how much the guy knew who said "Laughter is the best medicine." HOO HAH!

It is possible, of course, that he meant "Laughter is the best *tasting* medicine." This really shows you what a nudnick he was! I know of some much more daring medicines. I know of a

[2]·You may like it but you won't get it, it's in another collection. What do you expect for 35¢ anyway?
[3]·This joke is available on request.

cough sirup, for example, that tastes just like Manischewitz Wine when you pour it over the rocks. (It doesn't taste bad over ice, either.) Make this simple test at home: Pour first the cough sirup into a tall glass, then the laughter. See how much of a belt you get out of the laughter! I rest my case.

It seems pointless to go on because I think I have covered the subject adequately, and also because we are running out of paper. Those wishing to read the conclusion of my Backword will find it (with a fine magnifying glass) on the edge of this page in Sanskrit. The body of my message has been put across by now anyhow, which is simply that MAD is my favorite pastime (next to girls) and I hope you have enjoyed INSIDE MAD as much as I did. I boiled mine for dinner.

STAN FREBERG

"WOWEE, GANG—
I WISH I'D WRITTEN
BOTH THESE
NEW MAD BOOKS!"

—Charles Dickens

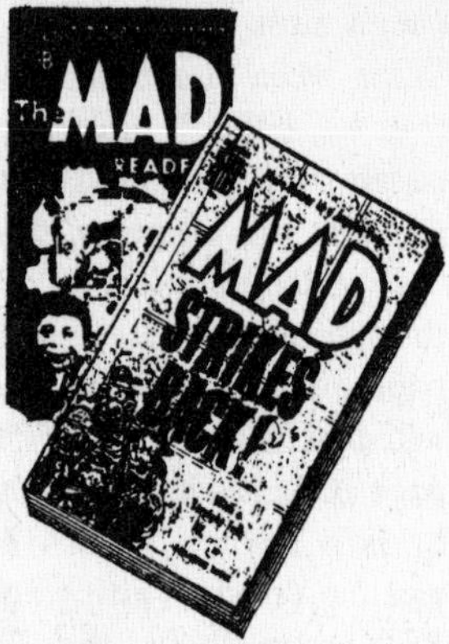

Yes, Charles Dickens of Mazzeppa, Long Island, is just one of thousands who have written in to say they wish they'd written The MAD Reader and MAD Strikes Back!

Now YOU can join the fun! It's easy! Here's how: —run right out to your neighborhood news stand and bring home a copy of The MAD Reader (only 35c). Look it over. Study the pages for the secret clues. Then run right back out to the news stand and buy a copy of MAD Strikes Back! (35c only). Now run right back home again—*fast!* Put the two books side by side and *watch closely*. You will see that they are *two different books!* If they are *three* different books, lie down for a half hour and then try again. On the other hand, if they are two copies of the *same* book it means you haven't been paying attention. We'll go through it one more time, slowly.

1. Run out and buy The MAD Reader (35c).
2. Run out *again* and buy MAD Strikes Back! (Another 35c).

Got it? O.K.—*start running!*

(NOTE: Many fun-loving MAD readers have run out to their local newsdealers and then got lost trying to run back home again. If lost, run to nearest mailbox and send 80c to the publishers, BALLANTINE BOOKS, 404 Fifth Avenue, New York 18, N.Y. They will send you both The MAD Reader and MAD Strikes Back! Of course you will still be lost, but now it will be fun!)

This publication, an exact reprint of Inside MAD *(1955), faithfully reproduces the advertisment above contained in the original. Readers are cautioned against relying on this advertising and should not consider any of it, or offers with it, valid in any way.*

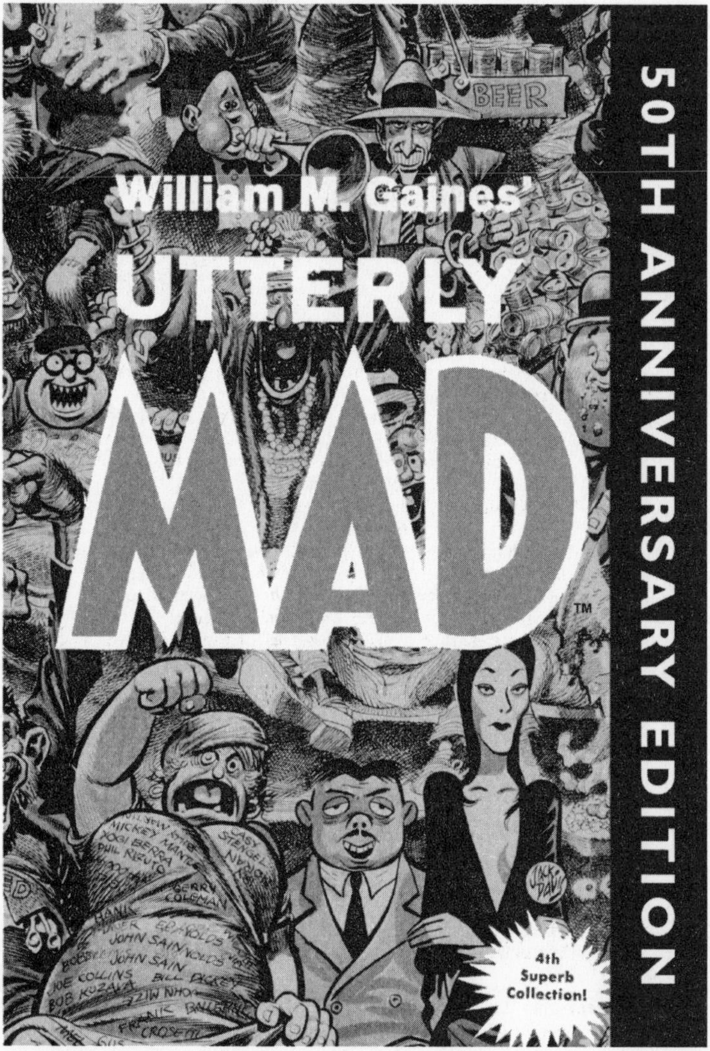
BEER
William M. Gaines'
UTTERLY
MAD
™
50TH ANNIVERSARY EDITION
4th
Superb
Collection!

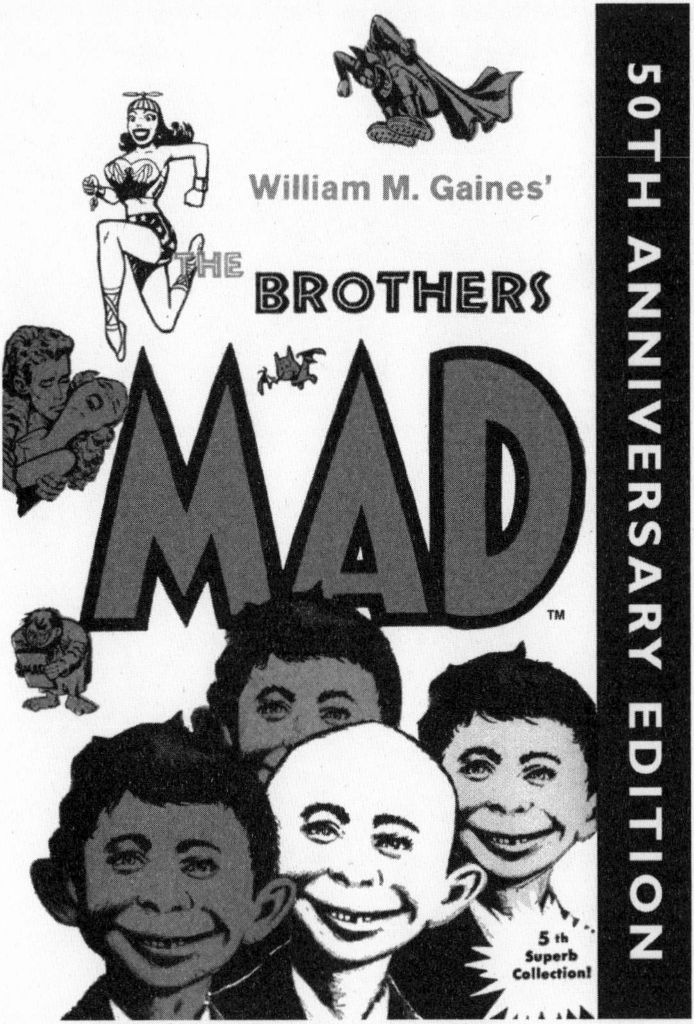
William M. Gaines'
THE BROTHERS
MAD
TM
5 th Superb Collection!
50TH ANNIVERSARY EDITION